Souvenir Post Cards

from

SHETLAND

Shetland in Picture Postcards

Compiled by
NORMAN HUDSON

The Shetland Times Ltd.
Lerwick
1992

First published 1992

ISBN 0 900662 82 4

Introduction and compilation © Norman Hudson

British Library Cataloguing-in-Publication Data

A catalogue record for this book is available from the
British Library.

Printed and published by
The Shetland Times Ltd.,
Prince Alfred Street, Lerwick, Shetland,
Scotland.

CONTENTS

INTRODUCTION
PICTURE POSTCARDS — A BRIEF BACKGROUND

The "Golden Age" of picture postcards in Britain occurred during the first decade of the twentieth century, largely coinciding with the reign of Edward VII. Postcard fever swept Britain and almost every household owned at least one album. Their geographic remoteness did not prevent Shetlanders sharing the national craze. "Another p.c. for your collection" is a message often found written on postcards from this time, even outnumbering references to the vagaries of the British climate. When the British later flooded to the seaside in their millions, the weather became an inescapable topic on many a holiday postcard!

Almost every aspect of life came to be depicted on picture postcards. Whether the collector's own interests lay in local scenes, music hall stars, cats, flowers or bicycles, the postcard publishers catered for all needs and, of course, endeavoured to stimulate new demands for their products. In the days before large-scale tourism and long before television documentaries, picture postcards of Shetland, for instance, could show a way of life appreciably different to the every-day experiences of friends and relatives living on mainland Britain.

The cards posted and collected in the Edwardian era were, however, quite different from the very first postcards, which had been produced over 30 years previously. The world's first postcard is generally recognised as that issued by the Imperial Austrian postal services in October 1869. These "Correspondenz-Karte" were plain and rather smaller than the postcards we associate with Edwardian times, but, largely because they could be posted at half the cost of posting a letter, they were instantly popular with the public. Other countries followed the Austrian example, the first British postcard being issued by the General Post Office just one year later.

The first picture postcards appeared in France in the early 1870s. Picture postcard production then gathered momentum throughout the 1880s and 1890s, largely through advances in printing techniques in Germany. The earliest picture postcards in Britain date from 1894. At the Post Office's insistence, the back of the card was reserved solely for the recipient's address and so the illustration — often little more than small engravings or line drawings covering only a section of the front of the card — had to share the front with a necessarily brief written message. These cards are known, logically, as "undivided backs", and it was not until January 1902 that the Post Office finally allowed the back to be divided in two — with the left side for the sender's message and the right for the address — allowing the whole of the front to be used for the illustration.

German influence in postcard printing remained very strong throughout the Edwardian era, with many British-published cards, including those with views of Shetland, being printed in, say, Saxony or Berlin. This ended when the Great War suddenly made the "Printed in Germany" inscription a hindrance to the postcard's sale.

The First World War largely brought an end to the "Golden Age" of picture postcard collecting. With the advent of a new era, with changed attitudes and priorities — and, arguably, with a loss of innocence — the national mood had altered beyond recognition. Postcards continued to be published, of course, but the era of mass collecting had come to an end. The legacies of this age now find the light of day from time to time, often when attics are sorted. These postcards are now sought after because they can provide a unique pictorial record of a moment in time frozen forever by the camera and of a way of life long gone.

INTRODUCTION
SHETLAND IN PICTURE POSTCARDS

The unique Shetland way of life has been well depicted since the earliest days of picture postcards. In the early years, for example, George Washington Wilson & Co. of Aberdeen produced postcards showing Shetland views largely photographed by Wilson himself (1823-1893) during his visits to the islands in the 1880s and early 1890s. This continued until the company went into liquidation in 1908. These early photographs are now preserved by the University of Aberdeen. Further, many nationally-renowned publishers, such as James Valentine & Sons of Dundee, featured Shetland views in their catalogues over the years.

Other photographers visited Shetland and made their own valuable contribution to the history of the islands' postcards. One notable example was Tom Kent (1863-1936) who had a shop in Kirkwall, Orkney, and whose legacy of photographs of Orkney itself is beyond compare in those islands.

In many ways it is the postcards produced by Shetland's own local photographers, sometimes in quite limited quantities, which arguably, provide the greatest interest today. In this respect Shetland has been blessed

POST CARD

FOR POSTAGE STAMP

POST CARD
BRITISH MADE

WALLS
A
30 JY
19
SHETLAND

SOUVENIR POST CARD

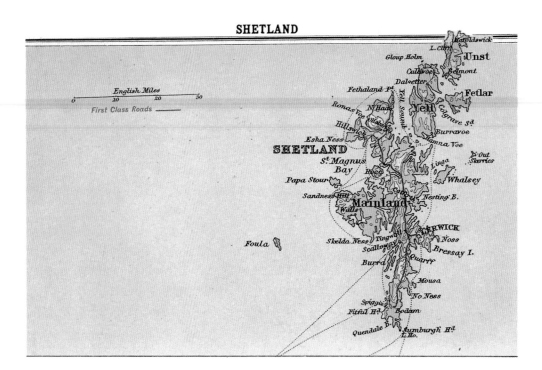

SHETLAND

2

— from the earliest days right up to the present — with photographers having an eye capable of capturing local views and lifestyles for picture postcard production. Several local names will feature in this volume. One of the earliest names to stand out is that of R. H. Ramsay of Lerwick. He originally contributed photographs to be printed as postcards by George Washington Wilson & Co. but, happily, several of these were subsequently reprinted under his own name.

In some ways, Shetland's own "Golden Age", in terms of postcard publication, occurred in the inter-war years with the work of J. D. (Jack) Rattar. Rattar's photographs cover practically every conceivable aspect of Shetland life, with the additional bonus that many of his sepia and white prints are veritable works of art. Jack Rattar's earliest photographs date back as far as the 1890s. In subsequent years his output of postcards and photographs was fairly prolific. In later life he lived in St Magnus Street, Lerwick, and kept a shop at 175 Commercial Street, at the foot of Back Charlotte Street. He was known as a kind and modest man and, when he died in 1957, he left a treasure-trove not only of his own work but also the photographs of others

which he had avidly collected over many years. Fittingly, the Rattar Collection was subsequently acquired by the County Library and this important and virtually priceless collection is now housed in the Shetland Museum for the benefit of all.

No acknowledgement of local photographers would be complete without mention of C. J. (Clement) Williamson who, happily, continues to sell postcards (including those featured in this collection) from his small wooden shop along the East Shore in Scalloway. To visit "The Studio" is truly to step back in time. Mr Williamson himself, though admitting to a ripe old age, has lost none of the keenness of mind and eye evident from his photographic postcards.

The work of several other Shetland photographers, not specifically mentioned in this brief introduction, is included in this volume. We are grateful to them, one and all, since, collectively, they have left us a comprehensive record of life in Shetland over the last hundred years, a legacy which many other parts of Britain cannot match.

Shetlanders.

1648. 1.

THE AUTHOR
"SOUVENIR POSTCARDS FROM SHETLAND"

Like many visitors to Shetland, I fell under the islands' spell on my very first visit. Soon afterwards I started to collect picture postcards not only as an armchair way of visiting the islands but also because I realised that the postcards themselves contained a vital pictorial record of a unique Shetland history slipping ever further into the past. The very first Rattar card I acquired was his superb view of the Reawick Regatta, a postcard reproduced in this book. I was instantly hooked! It is no coincidence that Jack Rattar's work features heavily in this volume. In this book I have endeavoured to bring together a selection of postcards to show a wide cross-section of the Shetland landscape and lifestyle. In preparing the accompanying text I have attempted to be informative without being too heavyweight. This, after all, is not intended to be a volume of local history. A number of publications by authors far better equipped to perform such a task are already available. The postcards selected are all from my own collection and, taken together, are intended to give a pictorial history of a part of the world treasured by many, either as home or a traveller's haven. In the future I intend to donate my collection of Shetland postcards and postal history to the Shetland Museum in the hope that it might give the pleasure to others which it continues to give to me. In the meantime, I dedicate this publication to the cherished memory of Edna Mary Hudson (1916-1991) who shared my love of Shetland and was the very best of travelling companions.

Norman Hudson, 1992

Norman Hudson

Norman Hudson was born near Wellington, Shropshire, in 1953. After graduating in 1974 with a BA degree in geography and history, Mr Hudson took up a local government administrative post with a district council near Chester where he has worked and lived ever since.

His love of travel led to many holidays spent exploring the islands of Scotland. Shetland soon became his favourite destination and several holidays visiting the islands led to the start of a collection of Shetland postcards and postmarks which now numbers several thousand items.

BRITAIN'S NORTHERMOST POST OFFICE

- 1 JUL 1972

HAROLDSWICK UNST SHETLAND

WHALSAY 29 NO 10

LERWICK FROM TOWN HALL.

SUNSET, SCALLOWAY

GREETINGS FROM SHETLAND

SUMBURGH HEAD

MUCKLE FLUGGA, SHETLAND, BRITAIN'S FURTHEST NORTH

TRAVEL

TO SHETLAND BY SEA

Shetland's longstanding reliance on shipping for transport and communication links with the Scottish mainland is not easy to over-emphasise. Shetland itself provided what food and provisions it could but anything else required by the islanders had to be transported by sea. Yet, the islands were reliant on the services of whatever ships happened to be making landfall in Shetland and it was not until 1838 that a government contract was awarded for the first regular, weekly conveyance of the mails to and from Britain's northernmost island group.

1. 'THE NORTH COMPANY' ADVERTISEMENT CARD

The North of Scotland and Orkney & Shetland Steam Navigation Company — known as "The North Company" for short — produced this postcard in about 1908 to advertise its services. The company owned the St Magnus Hotel (built at Hillswick in 1900) and operated the 702-ton *St Ninian*, a ship which served Shetland from 1895 until the Second World War.

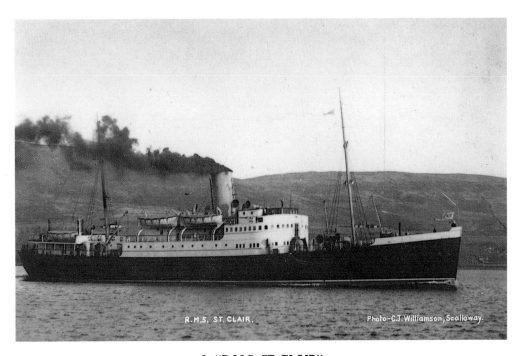

2. "R.M.S. ST CLAIR"

The 1,637-ton *St Clair*, launched in 1937, was the North Company's last steamship. Requisitioned by the Admiralty in 1940, the ship, renamed *HMS Baldur* for the duration of the Second World War, took part in the British occupation of the Faroe Islands and Iceland after the fall of Denmark. After the war, she returned to serve Shetland as a passenger ship until 1967.

TRAVEL
TO SHETLAND BY SEA

The 1,368-ton *St Sunniva* was perhaps the most striking passenger vessel ever to
have served Shetland. Built in Aberdeen, she was launched in April 1931, just a year
after the first *St Sunniva* was wrecked on the island of Mousa.

3. "R.M.S. ST SUNNIVA"
Photographed here at Lerwick's Victoria Pier in the 1930s, it is clear that the design
of the second *St Sunniva* repeated the distinct 'clipper' shape of her predecessor.
This decision has been called "a triumph of sentiment and beauty over utility".

4. "S.S. ST SUNNIVA, LERWICK"
Triumphantly bedecked in flags, the *St Sunniva* is about to pull alongside Victoria Pier.
During World War II, the ship was commandeered by the Admiralty. She survived
various assignments off the Norwegian coast but was eventually to be lost,
with all hands, off the coast of Nova Scotia in January 1943.

For most home-comers or visitors travelling to Shetland by sea, Lerwick is still the first landfall. Shetland's ancient capital was at Scalloway but Lerwick — originally "leir vik", or "mud bay" to the Norsemen — took over this role in the eighteenth century. With a population of just 900 in the 1790s, Lerwick grew rapidly thereafter and housed over 2700 at the time of the 1841 census. Today, over 7000 of Shetland's total population of 22,000 live in Lerwick.

5. "LERWICK"

This multi-view postcard by Valentine & Sons not only shows several views of Lerwick but also Sumburgh Head and Bressay Lighthouse, views familiar to the traveller arriving by sea.

6. "LERWICK"

Lerwick's badge is featured on this card from "Valentine's Souvenir-Heraldic Series". The Burgh motto reads "Dispecta Est Thule" ("Even Thule was seen"), a reference to the words of Tacticus, biographer of the Roman leader Agricola who, sailing in northern waters, felt that he had sighted the northernmost lands of Roman legend. The photograph shows Lerwick Esplanade from the north.

LERWICK

Bressay Sound affords Lerwick a deep, natural harbour. This sheltered anchorage
was well known to Dutch fishermen who, as early as the seventeenth century, assembled
here each year for the start of the herring season. The town of Lerwick and
its harbour have steadily developed ever since.

7. "LERWICK FROM THE SOUTH"

A large warship rests at anchor in Bressay Sound. The island of Bressay (foreground) and the
rocky promontory of The Knab, with the distinctive shape of the walled burial ground
(centre left) are clearly seen whilst the town of Lerwick spreads out behind.

J. D. RATTAR,
PHOTOGRAPHER,
LERWICK,
SHETLAND.

8. "LERWICK FROM NORTH"

Viewed from the Hill of Greenhead (with Gremista Farm in the foreground), this view of Lerwick
shows the sheltering hills of Bressay in the background. Numerous fishing stations fill the har-
bourside where, in the mid-1970s, the purpose-built Holmsgarth ferry terminal was to be built.

LERWICK
THE WATERFRONT

In the days before the opening of the Holmsgarth ferry terminal, the traveller arriving by sea
would immediately be surrounded by the cosy but cluttered world of Lerwick's seafront.
The character of the seafront itself has been shaped by the town's past and emphasises
its traditional reliance on the sea for its links with the outside world.

9. "LERWICK FROM THE PIER"
This uncharacterically quiet scene at Lerwick's waterfront shows the turret of the
Grand Hotel (built in 1887) towering over the buildings fronting the Esplanade. Shop
names in evidence include D. Peterson and Laurenson Bros, the latter occupying
the same building as The Shetland Hosiery Company.

10. "SEA FRONT, LERWICK"
A peaceful scene at a busy Lerwick Harbour. The Queen's Hotel stands proudly at the left and
the characteristic clipper-bow of the *St Sunniva* shows clearly amongst the other vessels in the
days when the ships of 'The North Company' berthed in the heart of the town.

LERWICK
THE WATERFRONT

Over the years, reclamation of Lerwick's waterfront has led to the gradual loss of many characteristic features of the seafront. However, the town's 'South End' retains much of its original charm. One of the most prized features are the Lodberries, eighteenth century buildings with dwellinghouses fronting onto the street and, behind, storehouses with facilities for landing goods direct from the sea.

11. "LERWICK, A NORTHERN VENICE"
R. H. Ramsay's view of Lerwick's 'South End' captures the charm of this unspoilt part of the waterfront. A poem by Vagaland (T. A. Robertson) refers to Lerwick as "The Northern Venice" but in this case the description is probably the publisher's romanticism. The same inscription is to be found on postcards of Stromness, Orkney.

12. "A BIT OF OLD LERWICK"
This part of Lerwick remains unaffected by development. One of the characteristic Lodberries with its storehouse and waterfront loading bay, is prominent on the postcard.

LERWICK
THE HARBOUR

Lerwick Harbour has always been a busy place and still provides the focal point of the town.
The Victoria Pier was built in 1886 and extensions and reclamation works in the locality
have altered the appearance of the seafront at various times ever since.

13. "SOUTH ESPLANADE, LERWICK"

Valentine's printed this card for H. Morrison & Son of Lerwick in about 1910. Horses and
carts are busy bringing goods to the Victoria Pier. The eighteenth century Tolbooth (left
background) still had its clock-tower and spire (removed in 1927). Goodlad & Coutts' Boot
and Shoe Shop occupies the front-facing building (centre) at the Market Cross.

14. "LERWICK, LOOKING NORTH"

Lerwick photographer R. Williamson captured this harbour scene in the inter-war years. The
prow of the *St Sunniva* shows the vessel berthed at Victoria Pier and in what is now the
town's Small Boat Harbour, home of local boats, visiting yachts and Lerwick's lifeboat.

LERWICK
THE ESPLANADE

The appearance of the Esplanade has altered considerably over the years with land reclamation, the ever-increasing volume of traffic and with Victoria Pier now being used as a car park.

15. "THE HARBOUR, LERWICK"
It would not be recommended for pedestrians to stroll down the middle of the Esplanade today! This is now one of the busiest thoroughfares for traffic through the older part of the town. The building with the turret (centre) dates from about 1900 and was the office of The North Company. Today it is Leask's travel agency. To the left are the shop premises of J. & W. A. Herculeson, while the Albert Buildings (right, background) (also built in about 1900) face the waterfront.

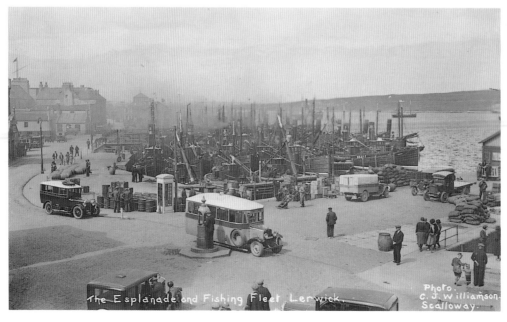

16. "THE ESPLANADE AND FISHING FLEET, LERWICK"
An industrious scene at the Esplanade with herring boats (mostly from Orkney and the ports of North East Scotland) crowding the harbour. The bus in the centre, standing by the Diana Fountain (erected in 1890) is owned by Leask & Son whilst the vehicle on the left is the bus to Scalloway. Perhaps the photographer, C. J. Williamson, travelled to Lerwick on this bus!

LERWICK
COMMERCIAL STREET

Commercial Street, as its name suggests, is where Lerwick's main shops, banks, post office and business premises are to be found. The street winds to follow the line of the adjacent waterfront. With many of the shop premises showing their gable-end to the street frontage, Commercial Street's shop fronts display a bewildering variety of angles.

17. "COMMERCIAL STREET, LERWICK"

J. D. Rattar captured the flavour of a busy day in the town's main thoroughfare. Peter Leisk & Co. (the shop with the white awning) were "Fruiterers, Florists and Confectioners". T. J. Anderson's shop (right) advertised newspapers. Today it is the tourist information office. Laing's pharmacy (background) is still there today.

18. "COMMERCIAL STREET"

The Grand Hotel, at 145-151 Commercial Street, was built in 1887 and occupies a focal point of this part of the thoroughfare. The premises of J. L. Pole occupy the shop immediately opposite the entrance of Pilot Lane, one of the innumerable steep lanes leading off Commercial Street on its landward side.

LERWICK
COMMERCIAL STREET

When Sir Walter Scott visited Lerwick in 1814 he observed that "the streets (are) flagged instead of being causewayed, for there are no wheelcarriages". The stone flagstones of Commercial Street were originally quarried on Bressay and, later, on Mousa but are now largely concrete replacements. If the modern visitor assumes Commercial Street to be pedestrianised, the sudden confrontation with a car or van can be a sobering experience!

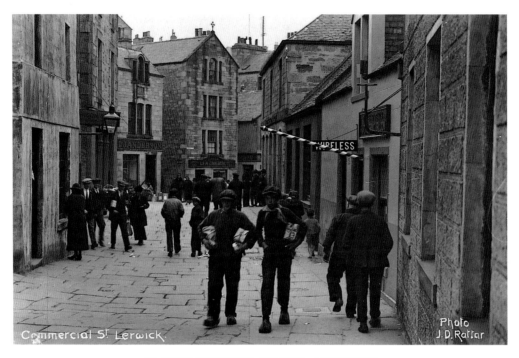

19. "COMMERCIAL STREET, LERWICK"

J. D. Rattar's photograph has caught what would appear to be two young Dutch boys (in clogs), possibly carrying parcels for posting at the post office just a few yards behind where the photographer stood. Shop names in evidence are T. J. Anderson (now the tourist information office) and J. & M. Linklater (both left background) while the wall-mounted sign above the barber's pole advertises "Ladies and Gents Hairdressing Saloon" on the premises belonging to R. Williamson at 56 Commercial Street.

20. "SOUTH END, LERWICK"

The "South End" in question is the southern end of Commercial Street. The Queen's Hotel (dating from the 1860s) is on the right whilst the building to the rear is the Tolbooth (built in the 1760s). The latter has served over the years as court-room, prison and custom-house. Its distinctive clock-tower had been removed in 1927.

LERWICK
CIVIC PRIDE

The late Victorian era saw an outbreak of civic pride which led many British towns and cities to erect magnificent civic builtings. This movement did not leave Lerwick itself unaffected. However, in a town of only 4800 people (in 1901) even if the manifestation of civic pride was understandably not of the scale of cities on the mainland, the results were nonetheless striking.

POST OFFICE, LERWICK.

21. "POST OFFICE, LERWICK"
Lerwick's earliest post office had been founded in 1763. The present post office building at 46-50 Commercial Street was built in 1910 and occupies a prominent position in the street scene, appropriate to its outstanding design. We can only speculate about how many postcards have been posted here over the years!

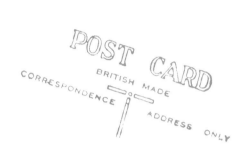

LERWICK TOWN HALL AT MIDNIGHT.

22. "LERWICK TOWN HALL AT MIDNIGHT"
This early "undivided back" postcard, posted at Lerwick in July 1903, is something of a novelty in that the photograph of Lerwick's magnificent Town Hall was taken at midnight, showing that Shetland's famous "Simmer Dim" — when summer's daylight is virtually continuous — allows photographs to be taken even at the witching hour.

Dear Joann, We got your P.C. this morning: you do send such nice ones. You may not be interested in the Lerwick town hall, but the fact that the photo was taken at midnight may remind you of the summer nights you spent in Shetland.
Your loving cousin
Mimie.

LERWICK
TOWN HALL AND WAR MEMORIAL

Lerwick's Town Hall and the Shetland War Memorial occupying fittingly prominent positions on Hillhead, at the head of the town. The Town Hall can be seen from many parts of Lerwick and seems to dominate the town when seen from ships arriving at or departing from the harbour.

FOR POSTAGE STAMP
Printed in Germany.

Lerwick Town Hall, and War Memorial.

Photo – R. Williamson

23. "LERWICK TOWN HALL AND WAR MEMORIAL"
The Town Hall was built in 1884 and was designed by the architect of Inverness Cathedral. Its construction represents a true outbreak of Lerwegians' civic pride. Architect Mike Finnie aptly describes the Town Hall as "rising high above the town like some Flemish cloth hall". The building incorporates magnificent stained-glass windows depicting characters from Shetland's history.

Unveiling The Shetland War Memorial at Lerwick, 6th January, 1924.
Photo: by R. H. Ramsay.

Ramsay Ph. Lerwick

24. "UNVEILING THE SHETLAND WAR MEMORIAL AT LERWICK"
A large crowd assembled in Hillhead to witness the ceremonial unveiling of Shetland's War Memorial on 6 January 1924, the Memorial itself occupying an appropriate position outside the Town Hall. The land in the middle distance on the left was to be the site of the Shetland Museum and Library (built in 1966).

LERWICK
THE 'NEW TOWN'

Lerwick's 'New Town' — on land to the west of Hillhead — started to grow in the late 1870s as a reaction to the crowded and, at the time, often slum-like housing conditions in the network of narrow lanes rising steeply from Commercial Street. The herring boom of the 1880s, and the wealth it created, provided an enormous impetus to development west of Hillhead.

25. "LERWICK FROM THE TOWN HALL"

This early view of Lerwick's developing New Town, seen looking north-west from the Town Hall tower, shows the Zetland County Buildings and the Police Station (in the foreground). Built in 1875, these were the earliest buildings in this part of Lerwick. A regular grid-iron of streets was eventually to be laid out but, originally, High Street ran diagonally between Hillhead and Commercial Road until its line was lost beneath the regular pattern of St Olaf Street and King Harald Street (seen running parallel to the left of this photograph).

26. "LERWICK LOOKING NORTH"

An identical view pictured some years later shows further developments in this part of the town. Most notably, this includes St Clement's Hall (built in 1911). This fronts onto St Olaf Street and faces the King George V Playing Fields. The playing fields are the site for the ritual burning of the Up-Helly-A' viking ship each January.

LERWICK
VIEWS FROM THE TOWN HALL

The clock tower of Lerwick Town Hall is still accessible to visitors at opening times and is well worth the effort for the magnificent panoramic views it affords of all parts of the town.

27. "NORTH HARBOUR, LERWICK"
Viewed from the Town Hall tower and almost directly north, Market Street is seen running down to meet Commercial Road. The stoutly walled garden in the left foreground, adjacent to the County Buildings and the Police Station, served as the prison yard.

28. "LERWICK FROM TOWN HALL"
Viewed looking in a south-easterly direction, the rooftops of Lerwick cluster on land sloping steeply down to Commercial Street and the harbour. Victoria Pier and today's Small Boat Harbour seem deceptively quiet from this distance. The island of Bressay (in the background) has provided shelter to Lerwick Harbour since Bressay Sound and Lerwick's waterfront was first used as an anchorage.

Following the development of Lerwick's 'New Town' in the later years of the nineteenth and the early years of the twentieth century, Burgh Road was to be the town's boundary until 1938. Many substantial villas lined the new residential streets which, reflecting the revival of interest in Shetland's Norse past at this time, were frequently given the distinctively Scandinavian names we see on the town plan today.

29. "LERWICK FROM TOWN HALL — LOOKING SOUTH WEST"
Looking towards Breiwick and the Ness of Sound the focal point of R. H. Ramsay's photograph is the Central Public School in King Harald Street. To the extreme right of centre is Islesburgh House (built in 1907), now a youth hostel. The houses in the foreground (with their backs to the camera) face on to St Olaf Street and the open space of what was to become King George V Jubilee Park. The site where the washing line stands (left foreground) is now occupied by the Shetland Museum and Library.

30. "CENTRAL PUBLIC SCHOOL, LERWICK"
The distinguished building of the Central Public School opened for use in 1902, with separate entrances for boys and for girls. Today this magnificent building serves as the Islesburgh Community Centre. During the summer months an exhibition at the centre provides fascinating insights into Shetland life.

LERWICK
THE LANES

The network of narrow lanes climbing steeply between Commercial Street and the higher ground of Hillhead, is a characteristic feature of the Lerwick townscape. After Commercial Street itself, the lanes — generally called "Closses" — were the earliest areas of Lerwick's residential development and, for a long time, had become the town's slums. Large areas were demolished in the 1960s and 1970s but later, as in many other towns and cities, renovation and conservation became the keywords.

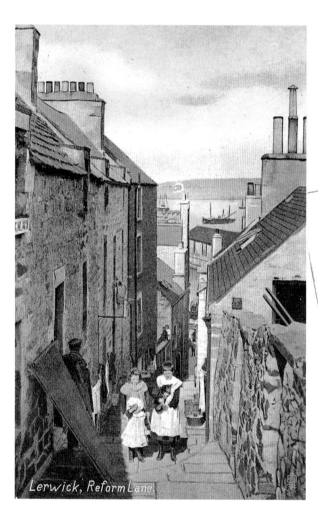

Lerwick, Reform Lane.

31. "LERWICK, REFORM LANE"
This early "Chromette" postcard by Raphael Tuck & Sons was "specially published for H. Morrison & Son, Lerwick" and shows housing in Reform Lane. Originally called Tait's Closs — named after Gilbert Tait, a local merchant and fishcurer — this narrow lane was re-named in 1845 after the Reform Act of 1832.

32. "BANK LANE, LERWICK"
This view of Bank Lane, printed in postcard form by The Shetland Times Limited, gives a good impression of the steepness of the lanes sloping up from Commercial Street to Hillhead. Anyone who has ascended the lane will realise how necessary the handrails really are!

The short distance from Commercial Street out to The Knab via Twageos Road will give the walker not only a relaxing ramble and interesting views over Bressay Sound but also close-up views of two particularly fine buildings associated with the life and work of Shetlander Arthur Anderson (1792-1868), MP for Orkney and Shetland between 1847 and 1852 and, in 1837, co-founder of the Peninsular Steam Company, later the Peninsular & Oriental Steam Navigation Company (P&O).

Widows Homes, Lerwick.

33. "WIDOWS' HOMES, LERWICK"
The Widows' Homes (now known as the Anderson Homes) in Twageos Road were built in 1865 as almhouses for seamen's widows. There were the gift of Arthur Anderson in memory of his wife.

ANDERSON E. INSTITUTE, LERWICK

PHOTO J. D. RATTAR

34. "ANDERSON EDUCATIONAL INSTITUTE, LERWICK"
Now known as the Anderson High School; the Educational Institute was founded by Arthur Anderson in the early 1860s and represents the benefactor's single most important gift to the islands. The school's motto "Doe weel and persevere" were the words spoken to Anderson when he left Shetland to join the Royal Navy

LERWICK
DUTCH FISHING SEASON

The natural advantages of Lerwick Harbour have long been recognised by fishermen. The Dutch were paramount in the earliest commercial exploitation of Shetland's herring fisheries and, in the early eighteenth century, it is said that the Dutch fleet occasionally numbered 2000 vessels. Dutch fishermen remained a familiar sight in the Lerwick street scene until the early years of the twentieth century. Remaining as cosmopolitan as ever, Lerwick is still visited by fishermen, mariners and tourists from all nations.

Dutch Fishing Season.　　　　　　　　　　*A quiet stroll at Lerwick.*

35. "DUTCH FISHING SEASON — A QUIET STROLL AT LERWICK"
The two Dutchmen pictured are strolling along Commercial Street. Perhaps they are heading for the shop in the centre right background, now The Shetland Times bookshop!

Ramsay, Photo., Lerwick　　　　　　　Dutch fisher boys at Lerwick

36. "DUTCH FISHER BOYS AT LERWICK"
The Feast of St John the Baptist (or Johnsmas) on 24th June traditionally signalled the start of the herring season in Shetland waters by which date the Dutch sailing vessels would be assembled to fill the wide stretch of Bressay Sound.

LERWICK
UP-HELLY-A'

Up-Helly-A', celebrated annually on the last Tuesday in January, is a comparatively new festival in its present form but can be traced back to the celebration of 'Uphalliday', one of the pagan Norse festivals adopted by the pre-Reformation Church of Scotland to mark the end of the long mid-winter celebration of Yule. The burning of a replica viking galley is the spectacular highlight of this popular festival.

37. "UP-HELLY-A' WAR GALLEY AND CREW"
The Norse associations of much of the Up-Helly-A' celebrations were strengthened in the later years of the nineteenth century. The festivities, presided over by guizers in replica viking costumes, stress the links between modern-day Shetland and the islanders' Norse ancestors.

38. "UP-HELLY-A"
A torchlight procession, as featured in this 1950s postcard published by The Shetland Times Limited, has been an integral part of the Up-Helly-A' festivities since 1881. The procession accompanies the replica viking galley to Lerwick's King George V Playing Fields where the galley itself is set ablaze with the fire from the guizers' torches.

Shetland's dead numbered over 500 in the First World War, a greater proportionate loss of life than suffered by any other county in Britain. Shetland played its full part, too, in the Second World War with Sullom Voe providing the site for an RAF base and the islands providing the initial safe haven for most of the 5000 Norwegian escaping from their occupied country. By the end of the war the loss of a further 300 Shetlanders was mourned.

39. "BOMB CRATER FROM FIRST ENEMY ATTACK ON SHETLAND"
When the Second World War began in September 1939, it was widely expected that London and the South-East of England would be the target for the first air attacks. But, perhaps surprisingly, it was Shetland that experienced the first attacks by German aircraft. The first bombs were dropped on Shetland on 13th November. Mercifully, there was no loss of life.

40. "SULLOM VOE DURING THE WAR"
During the Second World War, an airfield, used by Coastal Command patrol planes, was established on the south-east side of Sullom Voe. The airfield (at Scatsta) is today largely used in connection with the giant Sullom Voe Oil Terminal built nearby. The oil terminal was built on land to the right background of this photograph and was officially opened by H.M. Queen Elizabeth II in May 1981.

SHETLAND IN LOVE

Shetlanders in love were probably no different to anyone else in the rest of Britain. However, the Edwardian era was an age only slowly emerging from Victorian prudity and many picture postcards gave the writer an opportunity to send a rather risque greeting to his or her friends.

Shetland Courtship.

41. "SHETLAND COURTSHIP"
With the two lovers hidden from public gaze by the peat-stack, decorum is further preserved by the straw kishie placed over their heads!

42. "A SHETLAND KISS ON THE SLY"
Managing to ignore the postcard's subject, the writer asks, "You might send up some fine weather if you have any to spare".

A Shetland kiss on the Sly.

The development of the traditional Shetland dwellinghouse from the old Norse long-house is quite easy to see. In early years the single entrance was shared by both the family and their cattle. Although considered insanitary from our modern viewpoint, the arrangement not only sheltered the house but also allowed the crofters to tend the cattle without having to be concerned about the severe weather outside.

43. "SHETLAND CROFTER'S HOUSE"

At one time the roof of most Shetland homes were thatched. Overlapping turf was covered by a thick layer of straw. Ropes of twisted heather, secured with large stones, then held the whole in place against the worst of the Shetland weather. The best example of a traditional dwelling-house remaining today can be seen at the Shetland Crofthouse Museum at Dunrossness.

44. "A CROFTER'S HOME"

J. D. Rattar photographed this substantial crofter's house at Norwick on the island of Unst. With easy access to the beach, the location of the dwellinghouse shows the age-old dual dependence of Shetlanders on the land and on the sea.

SHETLAND AT HOME
THE SHETLAND CROFTHOUSE

At the 1901 Census, Shetland's population stood at 27,700. Of these, 4800 lived in Lerwick whilst the remainder lived largely in the scattered crofting communities throughout the islands. The crofters themselves gained a hard-earned living from the land and the sea.

45. "A DELTING CROFT"
At the 1931 Census — roughly when J. D. Rattar's photograph was taken — the population of the Mainland portion of Delting Parish, centred on Brae, stood at 800, significantly less than half the population when it reached its peak in 1851. Rural depopulation has been a serious problem for Shetland for many years but is certainly not a problem unique to Shetland itself.

46. "INTERIOR SHETLAND CROFTERS COTTAGE"
R. H. Ramsay's fine study shows many elements typical of life in a Shetland crofthouse. The family relaxes round the open peat fire but the women's hands are never idle. The room is flanked by two box beds — essential for keeping out the drafts. Dried, salted fish hang from the rafters and will provide a source of food during the winter months.

SHETLAND AT HOME
YOUNG SHETLANDERS

School education became compulsory in 1872 and free in 1889 but poor school attendance continued to be a problem throughout Shetland. This was largely due to the islands' poor roads or, often, their complete absence. Parents were understandably reluctant to send young children to a school several miles away over bleak and exposed hills. Yet evidence suggests that Shetland children's educational attainments were often higher than average.

47. "PEERIE SHETLANDERS"
Although four of the peerie (small) Shetlanders in R. H. Ramsay's photograph are wearing substantial shoes, two are wearing rivlins, the traditional shoes made of sealskin or cow-hide. The young boy on the right is bare-footed.

48. "YOUNG PEAT WORKERS"
Even at play, these two young Shetlanders are learning lessons for later adult life. The boy is putting peats into a small kishie whilst the girl, even at her tender young age, has obviously learned knitting skills from her elders.

A crofter's boat was exceptionally important to the livelihood of his family. The hard-won fruits of the sea could be added to the hard-won fruits of the land to eke out the family's resources.

49. "AT THE NOOST"
When not in use, the crofter's boat would be kept in a "noost", a hollowed-out shelter above the high-water mark. It is thought that this photograph by J. D. Rattar, of a crofter working on his fishing boat, was taken on Foula.

50. "GROUP OF FAIR ISLE FISHERMEN"
The "haaf" (deep sea) fishing was once the principal source of income on Fair Isle until the decline of this trade in the late-nineteenth century. Since then, fishing on Fair Isle has been largely inshore, mainly for saithe and haddock and, in recent years, for lobsters. This photograph dates from about 1900.

A LIVING FROM THE SEA
THE HERRING INDUSTRY

The Dutch had fished Shetland's herring grounds, perhaps the richest in the North Sea, since the sixteenth century. British attempts to exploit the trade had met with limited success until, in the late 1870s, new markets in Germany and Russia gave a tremendous boost to the development of the herring fishery in Shetland waters.

51. "RUSHING TO CATCH THE MARKET"
Shetland's herring catch reached its peak in 1905. In that year almost 1800 vessels landed their catch in Shetland, 300 of these being sailboats owned by Shetlanders. From about 1900 onwards, the sailboats were supplanted by steam-powered vessels which had first made their appearance in the ports of East Anglia and which, because of their greater range and speed, soon came to dominate the industry.

52. "A GOOD CATCH OF HERRING"
The steam-powered vessels were much more expensive to purchase and operate than most of Shetland's crofter-fishermen could afford. Of the 310 British steam drifters based at Lerwick in 1910, only eight were owned by Shetlanders. The letters "LK" indicate that the vessel in J. D. Rattar's photograph was registered at Lerwick itself.

A LIVING FROM THE SEA
"HERRINGOPOLIS"

From about 1880 until 1914 Shetland dominated Northern Europe's herring industry.
Boats from Shetland mingled with boats from the rest of Scotland, from Northern England,
Ireland, Holland, Germany and Scandinavia. Shetland soon came to be known as
"Herringopolis" and the industry came to dominate the islands' economic life.

53. "THE FISHING QUARTER"

Lerwick retained the title of Britain's main herring port for many years. Popular
legend would have it that, at the industry's peak, the fishing vessels were assembled
in such great numbers that you could walk from Lerwick to Bressay across their decks.
This photograph, looking across the fishing stations of Gremista and North Ness,
shows the legend to be not too far from the truth.

54. "PART OF THE FISHING FLEET"

The herring industry brought money to finance the expansion of Lerwick. Victoria Pier,
pictured here with the fishing fleet at rest, had been built in 1886. Although the industry
declined fairly rapidly after the peak year of 1905 and was to be seriously disrupted by the
First World War, it revived temporarily after 1919 and between 300 and 400 steam drifters
continued to operate from Lerwick for some years. This photograph dates from about 1925.

A LIVING FROM THE SEA
"KING HERRING"

In 1906 over 190 herring curing station were operating throughout Shetland.
No fewer than 40 of these were located in and around Lerwick which became the
islands' main base for activity between mid-July and September. The curing stations
crowded the shoreline westwards and northwards from North Ness.

55. "GREMISTA, LERWICK"
Gremista, photographed here from North Staney Hill, housed several of Lerwick's
busiest herring curing stations. The firms of E. Gordon and J. W. Plant & Son have both
proudly painted their names on the roofs of their respective premises. In the foreground
are some of the huts used to accommodate the itinerant workforce.

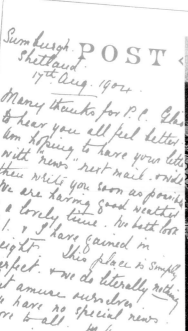

56. "FISHING STATION, SKIBADDOCK, LERWICK"
This early view of a herring curing station shows storage space for the countless
packed and unpacked wooden barrels to be at an absolute premium. Sailboats
fill the anchorage but, tellingly, the existence of a steam-powered vessel signifies the
beginning of the end for the sailboat's domination of the herring fishery.

A LIVING FROM THE SEA

"KING HERRING"

At the peak of the herring industry in Shetland, in 1905, a fleet of almost 1800 vessels landed a total of 645,000 crans of herring in the islands (a cran being three and a half hundredweight). Well over one million barrels of herring were cured, worth in excess of half a million pounds. Even during the years after the First World War, between 200,000 and 300,000 crans continued to be landed annually in Lerwick.

57. "LANDING THE CATCH"

In 1905, well over 12,000 men were directly employed in the herring fishing fleet in Shetland waters. Many were from England and mainland Scotland but about 2000 were Shetlanders.

58. "HERRING STATION AT WORK"

During the boom years Shetland witnessed a huge annual influx of female herring gutters and packers, together with all the other workers needed to process and handle the vast harvest of the herring shoals.

A LIVING FROM THE SEA
"KING HERRING"

The women who gutted and packed the herring were employed on a contractual basis.
A small payment, usually about one pound, was made to the woman by the employing
company during the preceding winter. Having "taken arles" as the saying went, the
women were then committed to work for the curing firm concerned.

59. " 'GUTTING', LERWICK"
Gutting the herring was the women's task. Men were employed at the curing stations but
largely as packers and, mindful of the enormous numbers of barrels needed, as coopers.

60. "HERRING GUTTERS, LERWICK"
The Shetland Times published this postcard in the late 1940s. It illustrated the fact
that although the herring industry declined in importance after the First World War, it
never completely died. In 1939 there were still 50 Shetland-owned boats involved in the
herring fishery. The Second World War was to take its toll of this number.

A LIVING FROM THE SEA

"KING HERRING"

All gutting and packing work was carried on in the open air. The deftness
of the women gutting, packing and salting the herrings was remarkable but the
unpleasantness of the work itself can only be imagined.

61. "A HERRING WORKER"

Shetland's herring season occurred during the summer
months. Shetland summers, however, can be notoriously
unpredictable and the women employed as gutters and
packers were obliged to cope with all weathers.

62. "SALTING HERRING, LERWICK"

It is not too difficult to imagine that the women's
work was demanding, back-breaking and not particularly
well-paid. The ever-present reek of the fish was
practically impossible to evade.

A LIVING FROM THE SEA
"KING HERRING"

The majority of the female gutters and packers came from the fishing villages and ports of the Moray Firth in mainland Scotland. They travelled to Shetland each year on the North Company's steamer, returning home when Shetland's herring season came to a close in September.

63. "HERRING GUTTING, SHETLAND"
The towering walls of the castle in the background show this photograph to have been taken in Scalloway, another of Shetland's main herring ports. This fine photographic study by C. J. Williamson gives a glimpse of the harsh and unpleasant conditions in which the women were obliged to work.

64. "INDUSTRIOUS FISHER GIRLS AT LERWICK"
Accommodation for the seasonal workforce was provided in the many huts erected at each curing station. These were often little more than sparsely-furnished wooden huts. As shown in this "Holmes' Silver City Series" postcard "specially printed for C. J. Duncan, Lerwick", even in their free time the women were seldom idle.

A LIVING FROM THE SEA
WHALING IN SHETLAND

Norwegian whaling companies received permission in 1903 to establish whaling stations in Shetland. This was shortly before whaling off the coast of Norway itself was banned because of over-exploitation. Two stations were opened in Ronas Voe in 1903 and two further stations opened in the following year, at Olnafirth and Collafirth.

65. "READY TO SHOOT THE WHALE — HARPOON SHOWN IN POSITION"
Although the plants provided local employment, there was much opposition to their existence. This was largely because of the stench and the pollution of local beaches. Anti-whaling demonstrations were held in Shetland in 1907.

66. "THE MOUTH OF A WHALE, OLNAFIRTH"
All whaling ceased during the First World War. Only the Hvalfang station at Olnafirth (west of the village of Voe) resumed operations after the War. Whaling zones around Shetland became increasingly exhausted until, by 1928, Shetland's whaling industry was extinct.

A LIVING FROM THE LAND

Whilst the sea was always of fundamental importance to the livelihood of the Shetlander, the land, too, was of equal importance. The family's croft, consisting of a simple stone house and a few acres of cultivable land, was the bedrock of the Shetlander's existence, allowing a subsistence-style level of agricultural production.

67. "WARM WORK — SHETLAND WOMAN HARROWING"
Shetland crofters were poor and their agricultural implements had of necessity to be simple and inexpensive. Perhaps nothing could be simpler — yet more physically demanding — than a harrow dependent on the strength of a woman's shoulders. Warm work indeed!

68. "PLOUGHING, FLADDABISTER"
A horse-drawn plough was a relatively uncommon sight in most parts of Shetland. Generally, only the larger crofts used ploughs since most crofts, being small agricultural units, could quite easily be tilled by spade. Fladdabister is a crofting township in the Cunningsburgh district where traditional methods survived longer than in most parts of Shetland.

Hairst (harvest) has always been the most crucial time in the crofting year. On its success depended the family's well-being throughout the winter ahead. A sudden gale late in the season could ruin the oat and bere (barley) crops and spell disaster for the entire district. Harvesting was itself a labour-intensive and laborious job. The work would often be done communally on the "many hands make light work" principle.

Herding Corn, Shetland

69. "HERDING CORN"
This early J. D. Rattar photograph was published in postcard format by H. Morrison & Son, Booksellers, Lerwick, and was known to have been taken in about 1900 at Benigarth, near the northernmost point of Mainland Shetland. "Hirding" was the word applied to the task of carrying the corn sheaves to build a larger "skroo" (corn stack).

A SHETLAND MEADOW.   Photo. J. D. RATTAR.

70. "A SHETLAND MEADOW"
J. D. Rattar's fine panoramic view shows a fruitful harvest scene. Innumerable desses of hay fill the landscape and cast long shadows on a fine, sunny Shetland day. The tranquility of the scene belies the hours of back-breaking human effort put into its production.

A LIVING FROM THE LAND
SHETLAND MILLS

Once harvested, the year's grain had to be ground to meal for the family's use through the long winter months. Horizontal mills (or "click mills", from the sound made whilst in action) were once a common feature in the Shetland landscape. Today, very few remain but their ruins can be seen throughout the islands. The mill's construction was simple but effective.

71. "SHETLAND CORN MILLS"
This mill — in good repair when the photograph was taken — stands on a sharp ravine carved by the stream which powers the mill itself. The ruins of a pair of mills, with one built slightly higher up the watercourse than the other, in a location very similar to this, can be seen at Funniquoy, near the Fair Isle Bird Observatory.

72. "AN OLD MILL"
One by one the traditional mills fell into disuse and disrepair. In this example, the roof has collapsed but, like many others, it is still easy to see the building's original purpose. The best preserved horizontal mill can be seen today at the Shetland Crofthouse Museum in Dunrossness.

A LIVING FROM THE LAND
GRINDING THE CORN

In addition to the water-powered mill — sometimes owned communally by groups of crofters — the harvested grain could be ground at home using a hand-operated quern. The quern stones can still be found today in the ruins of many abandoned crofthouses throughout Shetland. The main local grain crop was bere (a variety of barley) which, when ground, could be baked into bread or boiled with water to make porridge.

Shetland Mill, Interior.

Photo~ J.D. Rattar

73. "SHETLAND MILL, INTERIOR"
This photograph of a working mill shows the tapered wooden hopper, through which the grain was fed. The small shute at the base of the hopper was the "shü", designed to feed the grain into the millstone's central aperture. The wooden clapper fixed to the side of the shü rested on the millstone and was shaken by its motion. This caused it to strike against the shü causing it to vibrate and deliver a regular flow of grain.

THE QUERN   Photo J. D. Rattar

J. D. RATTAR, PHOTOGRAPHER, LERWICK, SHETLAND.

74. "THE QUERN"
The quern (a hand-operated mill) was still in widespread use at the beginning of the twentieth century. The photograph is of Johnny Clark of Skaw, Unst. The self-same quern and "looder" (the table on which the quern stood) is today part of the display material at the Unst Heritage Centre at Haroldswick.

A LIVING FROM THE LAND
SHETLAND CATTLE

As well as the grain and vegetable crops grown by Shetland's crofters,
there was also a traditional reliance on domestic animals. Cattle, sheep, pigs,
ponies, hens and geese were all contributors to the crofter's way of life.

75. "MOORLAND PASTURE"
The "kye" (cattle) were regarded as the crofter's most important livestock. The fresh
milk, butter and cheese were essential to the family's well-being. Shetland's own breed of
cow is quite small and is usually black and white in colour. It is well adapted to the Shetland
landscape and, importantly, the cows produce a relatively high milk yield.

76. "OXEN CARTS, FAIR ISLE"
Right up to the end of the Second World War, crofting techniques on Fair Isle
had remained essentially unchanged for many generations. Oxen were still used
on some Fair Isle crofts up to the early 1950s.

A LIVING FROM THE LAND

The crofter's land and the animals he kept could provide many of the essentials necessary to ensure the family's survival and well-being. Much of the working day of both men and women was, however, fully occupied with the many and varied tasks required on the croft and in the home.

SHETLAND "KIRNING".

77. "KIRNING"

This postcard is from Raphael Tuck & Sons' popular "Oilette" series, subtitled " 'Bonnie Scotland' — Life in Shetland". It shows the process of "kirning" (churning) which would take place in the home about once a week. Although the process was laborious, it produced both the family's butter and a kind of soft cheese known as "kirn milk".

Four Horned Sheep,
Lerwick.

78. "FOUR HORNED SHEEP, LERWICK"

Like the famous Soay Sheep of Scotland's Hebridean islands, Shetland's four-horned sheep also developed from relatively primitive goat-like ancestors. Being so dependent on their livestock in general, Shetlanders have traditionally shown great concern for the welfare of their animals.

SHETLAND SHEEP

It seems likely that the ancestors of today's breed of Shetland sheep were brought
from Norway with the early Viking settlers. The breed itself is relatively small but has
particularly fine wool. Sheep belonging to several local crofters would be allowed to graze
together on the scattald (the common hill grazings) but each crofter knew his own
animals by their lugmarks, the distinctive holes cut into the sheep's ears.

79. "SHETLAND LAMBS"
The sight of lambs is always a happy one because their arrival is a true harbinger
of the voar (springtime). Not surprisingly, it is also a time of hard work and anxiety for
the crofter whose livelihood, when the lambs are shipped south each autumn, can
be dependent on the success of the lambing season.

80. "CAAIN' SHEEP"
The sheep could mostly be left to fend for themselves on the scattald. But each year,
when it was time for the wool to be taken, the entire local community would cooperate to
"caa" or drive the sheep down from the hills and into the crö (the sheep enclosure).

SHETLAND SHEEP

Traditionally, the crofter's cattle were more important to the family's welfare than his sheep. But with the increase in demand for wool coupled with the increase in convenience shopping, the relative importance of cattle and sheep were reversed. It is estimated that the numbers of sheep in Shetland increased from 80,000 to 260,000 in the century after 1870 whilst the numbers of cattle fell from 21,000 to 7,000 in the same period.

81. "ROOIN SHETLAND SHEEP"
The removal of the sheep's wool by clipping is a relatively recent introduction in Shetland. In the Shetland breed of sheep the old wool naturally loosens under the new growth during the summer months and can then be "rooed" or gently pulled off by hand.

82. "SHEEP ROOING"
With the caa complete and the sheep assembled in the crö, the rooing could commence, traditionally in June. The natural colours of the Shetland breed of sheep range from black to white through varying shades of brown. The native breed of sheep has now been heavily inter-bred with imported breeds but the native sheep itself still has its supporters.

Knitting has long been an important element in Shetland's economy. The croft provided the family's basic food, warmth and shelter, and wages earned during the fishing season met the landowner's demand for rent. Knitting, however, provided not only some of the family's clothing but was also a source of ready cash to help buy those provisions or small luxuries which neither the croft nor the sea could provide.

83. "CARDING AND SPINNING SHETLAND WOOL"
Carding and spinning were the first two stages in the process of the making of the finished woollen garment. Carding (left) was usually undertaken using steel-spiked cairding boards. A small handful of wool would be repeatedly drawn across the cairds until, with all the fibres running in the same direction, the "rower" would be ready for spinning.

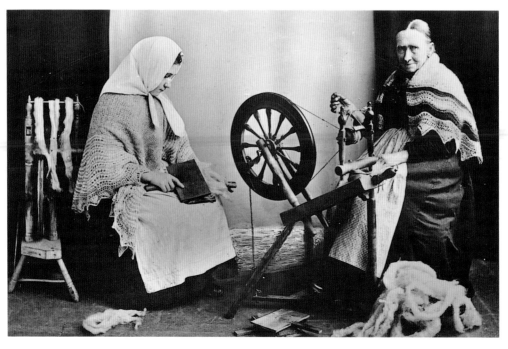

84. "CARDING AND SPINNING SHETLAND WOOL"
Carding and spinning were both time-consuming tasks. Such work, however, would always take second place to the needs of the croft and would be undertaken during quieter moments in the crofting timetable.

SHETLAND KNITWEAR

The spinning wheel is a prized possession in the crofter's home. It is not clear when the spinning wheel was first brought to Shetland but there are references to it in the early nineteenth century and its use was widespread by the middle of the same century.

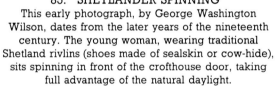
Shetlander Spinning

85. "SHETLANDER SPINNING"
This early photograph, by George Washington Wilson, dates from the later years of the nineteenth century. The young woman, wearing traditional Shetland rivlins (shoes made of sealskin or cow-hide), sits spinning in front of the crofthouse door, taking full advantage of the natural daylight.

86. "A SHETLAND SPINNER"
As with the carding process, spinning would often be undertaken communally by several women from the immediate neighbourhood. Their stories and laughter would turn duties such as these into pleasant social occasions.

SHETLAND KNITWEAR

Shetland knitwear is justifiably world famous. The comfort and durability of the
hand-knitted garments and the softness, delicacy and beautiful design of the hand-made
shawls and lace scarves of these northern islands are widely known. Whilst the demands
of the croft and the household occupied many hours, every spare moment of the
woman's day was devoted to her knitting.

87. "A SHETLAND KNITTER"

A woman's hands were never idle. Whether
tending the animals or carrying the peats home for the
fire, the woman's skilful and nimble fingers would
continually be at work on the "makkin", the name
applied to the knitwear being produced. This
photograph dates back to about 1885.

A Shetland Knitter

88. "SHETLAND KNITTERS"

This industrious and skilled group, known to be
Mrs Petrie and her daughters, are knitting Shetland
shawls, scarves and a sweater with an all-over Fair Isle
pattern. Fair Isle patterns probably survived from the
original Norse settlers. The pattern's popularity
spread when the Prince of Wales wore a Fair Isle
pullover to play golf at St Andrews in 1921.

Shetland Knitters

Photo ~
J.D. Rattar

SHETLAND KNITWEAR

A type of knitting known as Shetland lace developed from the extremely fine wool produced from Shetland's sheep. It seems likely that the craft developed from woollen copies of imported cotton lace but, whatever its origins, such garments came to be popularised by Queen Victoria after about 1886. By the turn of the century a fine Shetland shawl could command a price as high as £40.

89. "DRESSING SHETLAND SHAWLS"
R. H. Ramsay's photograph, dating from about 1910, shows hand-made Shetland shawls being pegged out on wooden frames in a Lerwick yard.

Sherland Hand Knirred Shawl.

90. "SHETLAND HAND-KNITTED SHAWL"
Shetland hand-made knitted shawls are known for their exquisite workmanship. Such knitwear is so fine and delicate that shawls such as this can be pulled through a wedding ring.

PEAT FOR FUEL

Peat, a material typical of cold, damp climates throughout the world, is one of Shetland's most abundant raw materials and has been dried and burned as fuel in the islands from the time of their earliest settlement. Most of Shetland is covered in a thick blanket of peat up to an average depth of about four feet.

CASTING PEATS.

Photo.
J. D. RATTAR.

91. "CASTING PEATS"
Early in springtime, the crofter would expose the peat banks by removing the covering layer of turf. These "faels", or slabs of turf, were used to cover the base surface of the "greff", the floor of the previous year's workings. The actual process of cutting the peat usually started in May.

92. "SHETLAND CROFTER CUTTING PEATS"
Shetland's traditional peat-cutting implement is a narrow iron spade known as the "tushkar". Deep, almost vertical cuts would be made and, with a deft flick of the wrist, the slabs are laid on top of the peat bank to form a dyke (wall), with regular spaces being left to allow the wind to pass through.

PEAT FOR FUEL

Peat-cutting can be hard, back-breaking work and was usually undertaken only by the men. Raising the peat, to aid the drying process, could then be left to the women or the children if the menfolk themselves were away at the fishing.

Peat Cutting, Shetland.   E. Sinclair.

93. "PEAT CUTTING"
The task of cutting proceeded until the crofter assessed that he had cut sufficient peat to last the family throughout the coming winter and right through to the next peat-cutting season.

94. "RAISING PEATS"
A short while after the peats had been cut, depending on the kindness of the weather in the intervening week or fortnight, the family would return to the peat-bank for the purpose of raising the peat, lifting the blocks manually from the dykes and forming them into small pyramids for the second stage of the drying process.

PEAT FOR FUEL

When the drying process was finally complete, the peats had to be carried back home using whatever methods were available. The tractor and trailer is now the normal sight but, in the past, peats could be transported by pony or, where appropriate, by boat. More commonly, however, they were carried manually.

95. "A SHETLAND PEAT CARRIER"
The most widely used method of carrying peat was the "kishie", a sturdy basket supported by a shoulder band. The kishie was traditionally made of straw ropes or "simmens" but such materials were to be replaced by imported cane.

96. "AGED 82. LANG MAY HER LUM REEK"
J. D. Rattar's photograph was taken in June 1934. Even in her old age, the Shetlander could seldom avoid the necessity of carrying home peats for the fire. The familiar reek of peat in the "lum" (chimney) meant that there was fire both for heating and for cooking.

PEAT FOR FUEL

All the peats required for the year ahead had to be transported home. This could often involve a lengthy and often-repeated walk across the moorland in travelling between the peat-banks and the crofter's home.

Shetland Peat Carrier.

Photo.
C. J. Williamson.
Scalloway.

97. "SHETLAND PEAT CARRIER"
Where the peat-banks and the home were not far apart, the peats could be stacked and protected where they had been cut. In this case the walk to the hill for a kishie of peats was part of the woman's daily routine. This feature was very much part of everyday life for women in Lerwick and Scalloway.

258.40.J.V.　　　A SHETLAND PEAT CARRIER.

98. "A SHETLAND PEAT CARRIER"
Typically, even with a back bent under the weight of a loaded kishie of peats, the woman knitted as she walked.

PEAT FOR FUEL

When the peats had all been transported home, the large stack built adjacent
to the dwellinghouse represented the fruits of about four months' intense labour.
Without the islands' massive peat supplies, life in Shetland would have been practically
impossible over the centuries. It is only in relatively recent years that alternative
sources of fuel have been available and, more importantly, affordable.

99. "SHETLAND PEAT CARRIERS"
The Orkney photographer Tom Kent is known for his sympathetic photographs.
Here he has managed to capture a flavour of the human effort and sheer hard work
involved in transporting the peats back to the crofter's home.

100. "STACKING PEATS"
The peats themselves, once transported home, had to be built into a weather-proof
stack. As shown in this postcard published by The Shetland Times, there were often
great skills exhibited in building such a stack.

PEAT FOR FUEL

Shetland's own native breed of ponies were at one time widely used throughout the islands to carry home the peats. The peats themselves were carried in nets known as "meshies" slung either side of a wooden saddle called a "klibber".

101. "BRINGING HOME THE PEATS, UNST"
When there were sizeable distances between the peat-banks and the crofter's home, it is not difficult to see that pony-power was preferable to the manual labour involved in transporting the peats in a kishie carried on the crofter's back.

102. "THE HILL ROAD"
With the gradual advance of road-building throughout Shetland, teams of ponies were slowly replaced by a wide use of horse-drawn carts. This photograph was taken at Lamb Hoga on Fetlar and it was on the island of Fetlar itself that the practice survived longest.

THE SHETLAND PONY

The Shetland pony (or the "Sheltie") is one of the world's smallest breeds of pony.
Its small size, stocky build and thick coat are direct results of the Shetland climate and
make the breed ideally adapted to its environment. It was widely used in Shetland to transport
peat and to carry seaweed, the latter being used to manure the crop-growing fields.

103. "SHETLAND PONIES BRINGING HOME THE PEATS"
R. H. Ramsay's photograph of Shetland ponies outside a traditional crofthouse was
originally published in postcard format by George Washington Wilson of Aberdeen.
After the latter company had ceased to operate in 1908, Ramsay subsequently
reproduced the photograph as a postcard under his own name.

104. " 'BY SEA AND BY LAND' — A SHETLAND STABLE"
Old boats can be seen in use as garage and shed roofs in various parts of Shetland. Here,
a former fishing vessel has been upturned for use as a stable for four Shetland ponies.

THE SHETLAND PONY

The average size of an adult Shetland pony is about 36 inches (nine hands).
The size of the breed itself, however, is variable and some can stand as high as 45 inches
(just over 11 hands). Their colours, too, are extremely varied, ranging from black to
light grey and varying shades of brown and chestnut.

105. "MINDING BABY"
A popular postcard in the Edwardian era showed
a crofter carrying a foal in his arms, emphasising the
extremely small size of the Shetland pony.

A YOUNG SHETLANDER IN ARMS.

Photo by J. D. Rattar, Lerwick.

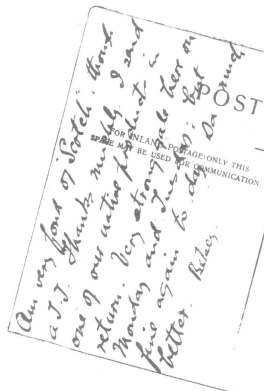

106. "A YOUNG SHETLANDER IN ARMS"
J. D. Rattar reproduced the "Minding Baby" postcard,
this particular card having been specially published for
George T. Anderson, the Lerwick stationer.

Prices for Shetland ponies rose rapidly after the early 1850s when the Sheltie was first exported to work pulling coal wagons down the mines of the British mainland. The price remained high for several years after the First World War but demand had collapsed by the early 1930s. Since that time, demand grew for Shelties as children's pets in Britain and on the continent.

107. "SHETLAND PONIES"
Largely because of their diminutive stature, Shelties are everyone's favourites. The Shetland Pony Stud Book Society was formed in 1890 to try to preserve the breed's purity.

108. "SHETLAND PONY AND FOAL"
Although their numbers in Shetland have fallen over the last century, Shetland ponies can still be seen throughout the islands. A particularly large number of Shetland ponies can today be seen on the island of Unst.

SCALLOWAY

Until overshadowed by Lerwick in the eighteenth century, Scalloway served as
Shetland's capital. The town's name is derived from the Norse "Skalavagr" (the bay
of the hall). After 1600, Scalloway was dominated by its great castle, built by Earl
Patrick Stewart and used by him to rule Shetland with an iron fist.

109. "GREETINGS FROM SCALLOWAY"
C. J. Williamson's 'multi-view' postcard shows five different views of his
home town. Scalloway Castle is centrally placed on the postcard, befitting the
domination of the town by these magnificent ruins.

110. "SCALLOWAY — FISHING FLEET READY TO START"
This photograph of Scalloway — said to be taken on a Monday morning — has been
substantially re-touched by hand, endeavouring to show that the harbour was busier than it
already was. Scalloway's cod trade was gradually replaced by haddock fishing and, in turn, by
herring. A new breakwater and a large fish market were built in Scalloway in 1983 and the
town is still very much dependent on the ups and downs of the fishing industry.

SCALLOWAY

Although Lerwick and Scalloway are only about five miles apart, the main contact between the two communities right up to the mid-nineteenth century was the 50-mile sea journey round the stormy headlands of the South Mainland. No road between Scalloway and Lerwick existed until 1874. Today the seven miles of road have been improved beyond all recognition. A sharp bend on the Scord affords a particularly fine view on the approach to Scalloway.

111. "SCALLOWAY"
This early "undivided back" postcard, by T. Mathewson, Lerwick booksellers, has a coloured drawing of Scalloway, as seen from the Scord.

Scalloway

Scalloway 4/4/02 a party of 7 of us have just driven over here (7 miles) + have had a look round, we are having a lovely day

Published by T. Mathewson, Bookseller, Lerwick

112. "SCALLOWAY FROM THE SCORD"
J. D. Rattar's view of Scalloway shows the town hugging Shetland's Atlantic coast and nestling at the end of the fertile Tingwall valley. It shows, too, how much the town is dominated by the castle's ruins. One of the North Company's passenger vessels is getting up steam at the pier. The town ceased to be a port of call when the 'West Side' steamer service ended in the late 1930s.

Scalloway from the Scord.

Photo
J. D. Rattar

SCALLOWAY

Scalloway's fortunes had declined at the same time as those of Lerwick had gradually risen. Despite this, many fine mansions were to be built in Scalloway in the eighteenth century by local lairds and, in the nineteenth, by prosperous local merchants. Many planted trees to enhance their homes. As a result, the town is particular photogenic and has featured on many picture postcards over the years.

113. "SCALLOWAY FROM WEST"
C. J. Williamson's fine panoramic view of his home town is photographed from Gallow Hill. As its name suggests, Gallow Hill was a place of execution. The last recorded execution was the burning in 1712 of the unfortunate Barbara Tulloch and her daughter, Ellen King, on a charge of witchcraft.

114. "EAST SHORE, SCALLOWAY"
The skyline is once again dominated by Scalloway Castle, towering over the rooftops of the old cottages in New Street. C. J. Williamson's photographer's shop, "The Studio", is situated along this stretch of the shoreline and so this view, looking down towards the pier, is very much on his home territory!

SCALLOWAY
SCALLOWAY CASTLE

Scalloway Castle was built in 1600 for Earl Patrick Stewart using forced labour.
He had succeeded to the title of Earl of Orkney and Lord of Shetland in 1593 and his
rule was harsh and tyrranical. Earl Patrick's behaviour proved to be his downfall. He was
arrested in 1609 and, together with his son, Robert, was executed in Edinburgh in
1615 on a charge of treason. The castle ruins dominate Scalloway to this day.

115. "SCALLOWAY CASTLE"
This postcard, showing Scalloway Castle from the north, was published by A. F. Inkster,
Scalloway. Alex Inkster ran a draper and hosier's shop in the town. He advertised that
"A complete selection of Local View Post Cards always on hand".

116. "SCALLOWAY CASTLE"
C. J. Williamson's fine photograph of Scalloway Castle gives a good impression of the original
grandeur of this tall, four-storey building. It was taken into the care of the state in 1908.

SCALLOWAY

Scalloway is well known as the former nerve-centre of the famous "Shetland Bus" operations during the Second World War. With Norway under Nazi occupation, Shetland was the base for an heroic and perilous operation shuttling supplies to the Norwegian underground and returning across the North Sea with refugees. The original base for the operation was at Lunna, on East Mainland, but the need for boat repair facilities led to Scalloway becoming the centre of operations.

117. "SCALLOWAY HARBOUR"
Winter scenes on postcards are comparatively rare since, if the publishers and tourist postcards are to be believed, skies are always blue and the sun is always shining! R. Smith's photograph shows a snow-bound Scalloway with the snow-clad fields of the island of Trondra and the hills of the South Mainland in the background.

118. "SCALLOWAY PUBLIC SCHOOL"
Scalloway school dates from 1876, having been built on the outskirts of the existing village. Under the auspices of Shetland Islands Council, the current Scalloway Junior Secondary School was developed in 1985 on an adjacent site.

SOUTH MAINLAND
SANDWICK

The area now generally known as Sandwick consists of several crofting townships — including Hoswick, Leebitton, Stove and Sandwick itself — spread over a large and relatively fertile central part of South Mainland.

119. "SANDWICK"
"Sandwick" is a common name in those parts of the British Isles influenced by the Norse invasion and settlement. The name simply describes a wide, sandy bay. J. D. Rattar's view shows a typically scattered township, characteristic of most parts of Shetland.

120. "HOSWICK"
The township of Hoswick largely consisted of a cluster of fishermen's cottages, neatly tucked in between the sea at the front of the hill to the rear.

SOUTH MAINLAND
LEVENWICK

Travelling south from Lerwick, the road hugs the hillside high above the
inlet called Channerwick and then skirts the township of Levenwick, the latter
occupying a picturesque position above a fine, sheltered, sandy bay.

121. "LEVENWICK"
J. D. Rattar's view of Levenwick township shows the modern road marching
northwards up the hillside on its way to Lerwick. Well-tended fields slope down to
the bay which was a favoured sheltered haven for Dutch fishing boats from the
earliest times. By reputation, it was also a haven for smugglers, too.

122. "LEVENWICK BAY"
This postcard was published locally by W. Leslie of Dunrossness and was posted
to Lucca in Tuscany (Italy). The photograph shows Levenwick's ancient, circular graveyard.
The gravestones in the foreground and the fishing fleet in the bay remind us of the
age-old perils faced by generations of Shetland fishermen.

Brochs are largely confined to the North of Scotland. Of the 500 known sites, 95 are in Shetland. Commonly known as "Picts' houses", brochs are massive fortresses, most probably built for the defence of the local population. At one time it was assumed they were built as a defence against the invading Vikings, but they are now known to date back to the Iron Age.

Picfish Brough, Lerwick.

Photo J.D.Rattar

123. "PICTISH BROCH, LERWICK"
Clickimin Broch, on the southern outskirts of Lerwick, is a complex archaeological site. A farmstead dating from 700-500BC was developed into an Iron Age fortress, the remains of which we can see today. The walls are up to 20 feet thick and, at one time, rose to a height of between 40 and 50 feet.

124. "BROCH OF MOUSA"
This Iron Age broch, situated on a low, rocky headland on the island of Mousa, is undeniably the best preserved of such fortresses in Britain. Dating from about 100BC-300AD, Mousa Broch rises to a height of 42 feet. It seems likely that its isolation has been its salvation since in many other archaeological sites throughout Britain stones have been removed to build houses or other structures.

SOUTH MAINLAND
SUMBURGH

Sumburgh Head is the southernmost point of the Shetland Mainland, situated approximately 25 miles from Lerwick. The dramatic cliff-scape of Sumburgh Head is an emotive sight to Shetlanders and visitors alike since it is the first — or last — point of Mainland Shetland seen from the passenger ferry sailing between Aberdeen and Lerwick.

125. "SUMBURGH HEAD"
Sumburgh Head itself is 270 feet high but appears much higher. Sumburgh Head lighthouse stands proudly on the headland. It was built in 1821 to the design of Robert Stevenson (grandfather of Robert Louis Stevenson) for the Northern Lighthouse Commissioners and was Shetland's first lighthouse. Like many other lighthouses, it has now been automated.

126. "LOOKING NORTH FROM SUMBURGH HEAD"
J. D. Rattar's panoramic view shows Sumburgh farmhouse (right, dating from the late seventeenth century) and Sumburgh House (left, built in 1867 and now a hotel). Jarlshof lies between Sumburgh House and the shore. The road northwards meandered across the flat area where, in later years, Sumburgh Airport was to be developed. The road itself was subsequently diverted to the west (left) and the current Sumburgh Airport terminal building was built on the site in 1979.

SOUTH MAINLAND

JARLSHOF

Jarlshof is an extraordinary archaeological site showing evidence of human occupation over a period of approximately 3000 years. The earliest part of the site is a Stone Age settlement. There are also extensive viking-age remains. The ruins of the seventeenth century laird's house on the site were given the name "Jarlshof" by Sir Walter Scott when visiting in 1814 and the name is now applied to the entire complex.

127. "EXCAVATIONS AT JARLSHOF"

Evidence of centuries of virtually continuous occupation of the site first came to light in about 1905 when a violent storm partially revealed the archaeological remains that we see today. The extensive site is comparable to the magnificent settlement of Skara Brae, in Orkney, revealed in about 1850 in much the same way as that at Jarlshof.

128. "JARLSHOF, SHETLAND"

The dry-stone building techniques of the pre-historic dwellinghouses had reached an advanced stage at Jarlshof. The interiors of these 'wheel-houses' were actually quite spacious, with small cells built into the walls, often for storage.

Much of Dunrossness, Shetland's southernmost parish, is characterised by scattered crofting communities, stretches of fertile agricultural land and beautiful coastal scenery. The parish's population reached a peak of 4500 in 1861 but has declined steadily since then to a level of about 2000 today.

129. "QUENDALE"
The township of Quendale lies in the lea of the massive cliffs of Fitful Head (928 feet). The Bay of Quendale (pictured) is fringed by a mile-long beach, one of the largest in Shetland. Quendale Mill was restored in 1990 as a working museum. J. D. Rattar's photograph shows the carpet of wild flowers so typical of a Shetland summer.

130. "IRELAND, SHETLAND"
The crofting township of Ireland, just to the north of Bigton, is thought to be named after the long sandy tombolo of shell sand, or ayre ("eyrr" in Old Norse) connecting neighbouring St Ninian's Isle to the Mainland. The foreground shows a typical Shetland homestead with turfed and thatched roof. The island of Foula (about 28 miles away) appears on the horizon.

The districts of Whiteness and Weisdale are deeply indented by long voes, or arms of the sea, running generally south-west to north-east. A magnificent view of the district is provided as the road from Lerwick reaches the top of Wormadale Hill.

131. "WHITENESS"
The road through Whiteness township occupies a narrow neck of land between the waters of the Loch of Strom and Stromness Voe. Today, a popular stop in the township is at Hjaltasteyn to see the manufacture of hand-crafted jewellery.

132. "KERGORD HOUSE, WEISDALE"
The crofting lands in the Weisdale valley were cleared to create a sheep farm after 1843, and over 300 people were forcibly evicted. Stones from some of the crofts were used to build Kergord House (called "Flemington" until 1945) in about 1850. Trees were planted in the late nineteenth century and grew successfully in the sheltered valley. Today, Kergord's trees provide an unusual sight in the generally tree-less Shetland landscape.

WALLS

The name "Walls" derives from the Norse "Vaas", "the place of voes", and a glance at a map will show the name to be entirely appropriate. The village, following the curve of the bay, was a place of some importance in the days of the great herring fishery. Walls boasts Shetland's oldest school, founded by the Society for the Propogation of Christian Knowledge as long ago as 1713.

133. "WALLS"
The village is the unofficial 'capital' of West Mainland and still has a number of large merchant's houses dating from the years when Walls was a more important centre than it is today. Walls has traditionally been the point of arrival and departure for the mailboat serving the island of Foula.

Packing Sillocks. Walls in Winter.

134. "PACKING SILLOCKS. WALLS IN WINTER"
The harbour at Walls is protected from the worst of the Atlantic storms by the islands of Linga and Vaila. During the winter months, when little other fresh food was available, sillocks (young saithe, or coalfish) were an important part of the local diet.

Much of West Mainland is a landscape of moorland and lochs and, as such, has always been sparcely populated. It has suffered heavily from the effect of rural depopulation. The westernmost Parish of Walls and Sandness, for example, had a population which peaked at over 1900 in 1861. One hundred years later it had declined to about 550.

135. "MID WALLS"

Mid Walls is a scattered crofting community due west of the village of Walls. The direct effects of the oil boom of the 1980s have made little impact on such townships. The characteristic outline of the island of Foula, about 14 miles away at this point, seems to float on the horizon.

136. "BRIDGE OF WALLS"

The "Bridge" in the name "Bridge of Walls" takes the main Lerwick-Walls road (the A971) across the head of the Voe of Browland. Its importance as a meeting point of several rural routes is reflected in the fact that a post office opened in this small township as early as 1884.

WEST MAINLAND
REAWICK

The main Lerwick-Walls road skirts the northern edge of Bixter Voe. The next turning left leads southwards to the communities of Garderhouse and Skeld. It leads, too, to the striking red sands of Reawick ("red bay"), long favoured as a beach for picnics and bathing.

137. "REAWICK"
This idyllic Shetland scene, looking south along Reawick's fine beach, was captured on a postcard by The Shetland Times. The sky is virtually cloudless, the road is empty, chickens scavenge for food and the washing on the line will undoubtedly be dry in no time at all.

138. "REAWICK"
In contrast to the quiet of the scene in the preceding postcard, J. D. Rattar's photograph of Reawick Regatta shows a hive of activity. The line of cars suggests that the participants have travelled from miles around. The scene is presided over by Reawick House, dating from the 1730s, with its strange castle-like outbuildings.

A minor road leading northwards from the main Lerwick-Walls road at Bixter
at first strikes across relatively featureless moorland but soon comes once again
to the sea. The coastline, like much of Shetland, is deeply indented and the
scattered communities of the district are well worth the detour.

139. "AITH"
The township of Aith lies at the head of Aith Voe. For many years the local menfolk often
found employment on the whaling ships. The seafaring skills and traditions of the township
was recognised when, in 1932, Shetland's second RNLI lifeboat station was opened at Aith.
Aith lifeboat serves the waters of the entire western coast of Shetland.

J. D. RATTAR,
PHOTOGRAPHER,
LERWICK.
SHETLAND.

140. "CLOUSTA"
Clousta is a remote but picturesque community at the head of the Voe of Clousta.
It is an area well known to anglers. A large hotel, essentially to cater for anglers, was
built at Clousta in 1895 but was destroyed by fire early in the twentieth century.

VIDLIN

Vidlin is an attractive township at the head of Vidlin Voe. It forms the
focal point of the Lunnasting district of the Parish of Nesting.

141. "CROFTS, VIDLIN"

J. D. Rattar's view shows a typical Shetland crofting community at a time
when most of the houses still had the traditional turf and thatch roof.

142. "VIDLIN"

Vidlin's crofts form a scattered community around the head of Vidlin Voe (left). There is
plenty of evidence from this photograph that the local crofters have had yet another industrious
summer in the well-tended fields sloping down to the voe and the adjacent loch.

The Parishes of Nesting and Delting occupy large areas of the north-eastern part
of Mainland Shetland. Much of the land is agriculturally poor upland moor, with a grandeur
all of its own. However, a number of scattered coastal communities maintain the
traditional crofting and fishing way of life of Shetland's rural districts.

143. "LAXO"

Laxo, a small township at the head of Dury Voe, today serves as the Mainland terminal
for the car and passenger ferry to Symbister on the island of Whalsay.

144. "TOFT. THE ROAD TO THE ISLES"

A coach awaits at Toft pier for the arrival of the ferry from Ulsta on the island of Yell.
The inter-island overland ferry route, linking the Mainland to Yell and Unst, began in
1932. The regular ship service between Lerwick and the North Isles, dating from 1839,
was ultimately to lose out to the faster overland route. The last of the North Isles
vessels, the *Earl of Zetland*, was withdrawn in 1975.

The main road north from Lerwick passes through the moorland wilderness of
Petta Dale before meeting the waters at the head of Olna Firth at the township of Voe.
Following the Atlantic coast, after a further few miles the road then reaches the narrow
isthmus of Mavis Grind, where the northern Parish of Northmavine is almost
physically separated from the remainder of Mainland.

145. "VOE"
Voe is strategically located at the 'crossroads' of routes to Lerwick, Hillswick, Toft,
Vidlin and Aith. Many comment on the Norwegian feel of the settlement at the head of
Olna Firth. It was an early base for the cod fishery and the home of Thomas M. Adie &
Sons, Shetland's oldest family business, with workshops producing Shetland tweed.

146. "MAVIS GRIND"
Twenty-five miles north of Lerwick, Mavis Grind ("the gate of the narrow
isthmus") is the point where the North Sea and the Atlantic are only a matter of
35 yards apart. Large-scale quarrying of Cliva Hill (centre) has now lessened
the dramatic effect of this section of the road to Hillswick.

NORTH MAINLAND
BRAE

The village of Brae lies between Voe and Mavis Grind at the head of Busta Voe.
Brae remained a quiet township until the oil-boom of the 1970s and 1980s when,
with the opening of the giant Sullom Voe Oil Terminal a few miles to the north-east,
much oil-related housing development transformed the settlement.

BRAE, SHETLAND.

147. "BRAE"
This anonymously-produced postcard shows the older part of the
township long before the advent of oil-related development.

U.F. CHURCH MANSE, BRAE, SHETLAND.

148. "U.F. CHURCH & MANSE, BRAE"
Brae Church and its substantial manse, seen mirrored in the waters of Busta Voe, still remain as
symbols of the settlement before the building of the Sullom Voe Oil Terminal a few miles away.

NORTH MAINLAND AND MUCKLE ROE

A side-road off the route between Brae and Mavis Grind leads southwards
to the hamlet of Busta. Shortly afterwards it reaches Muckle Roe, an almost
circular island first joined to the Mainland by bridge in 1905.

149. "BUSTA"

Busta lies on the west bank of Busta Voe, facing the village of Brae. It is the site
of Busta House, now a substantial and well-known hotel. Parts of the building date
from the 1580s but the main mansion was built for the Gifford family in 1714.

1d. STAMP
IF WITH ONLY
SENDER'S NAME
AND ADDRESS
AND 5 WORDS
CONVENTIONAL
GREETING H

PRINTED IN
GT BRITAIN

150. "A SHETLAND HEADLAND"

Although unidentified in J. D. Rattar's photograph, the headland in question is at North
Ham on Muckle Roe. The island is known for its striking red granite cliff scenery.

Northmavine is the northernmost Parish of Mainland Shetland. The land north of Mavis Grind is noted for its rugged grandeur, with large outcrops of red granite. The area has thin, relatively poor soils and, as a consequence, depopulation has had a harsh effect on the parish. Its population peaked at almost 2600 in 1861 but had fallen to about 800 a hundred years later.

151. "URAFIRTH AND RONAS HILL"
C. J. Williamson's photograph shows the main road from Lerwick winding northwards to the township of Urafirth (left), at the head of the voe of the same name. It is the final community before the road reaches Hillswick. Ronas Hill (1486 feet) is Shetland's highest hill.

152. "ARRIVAL"
The "arrival" in question is at Hillswick, the terminus of the 'West Side' steamer until the service ended in the late 1930s. Hillswick lacked an adequate pier and so passengers from The North Company's steamer had to be conveyed ashore by flit boat.

Hillswick became a destination for tourists from the earliest days. Visitors were drawn to this northern part of Mainland Shetland by the magnificent coastal scenery in the locality.

153. "HILLSWICK AND RONAS HILL"

This photograph was taken from the slopes of the Ness of Hillswick and shows the village of Hillswick in its location at the head of an arm of Ura Firth and dominated by the conical mass of Ronas Hill. St Magnus Bay Hotel (left) and the large white-painted Northmavine Kirk (dating from 1733) are prominent in the village.

154. "HILLSWICK"

R. H. Ramsay's view of Hillswick village, viewed from the beach, shows the extent to which the settlement is dominated by the St Magnus Bay Hotel (centre left) and Northmavine Kirk (centre right). Along the shoreline is The Booth, Shetland's oldest public house, dating from 1698.

Hillswick, 36 miles from Lerwick, is the natural centre for this remote northernmost
area of Mainland Shetland. By the time the 'West Side' steamer ceased to call at Hillswick,
the village was becoming the destination for road-borne trips by visitors.

155. "HILLSWICK HOTEL"
The St Magnus Bay Hotel was built in 1900 for The North Company for the
comfort of up to 60 cruise passengers. It was built in pre-fabricated timber sections
in Norway and shipped across the North Sea for erection at Hillswick.

156. "FRIENDLY OVERTURES"
Manson & Co. of Hillswick published this postcard showing a friendship
being struck in the sun-lit fields above Hillswick village.

NORTH MAINLAND
ESHANESS

Eshaness, about five miles west of Hillswick and at the extreme north-west of
Shetland's Mainland, has a dramatic coastline with awe-inspiring basalt cliffs.
Eshaness Lighthouse was built in 1929 and provides a magnificent viewpoint.

157. "GRIND OF THE NAVIR, ESHANESS"
The Grind of the Navir is one of the most striking features along the coast of Eshaness.
The name means "the gate of the borer", the "borer" in this case being the Atlantic Ocean.
The sea's ceaseless action has penetrated the cliffs to create this striking coastal feature.

158. "STENNESS, SHOWING DOOR HOLM"
The small crofting community of Stenness overlooks Dore Holm. This huge mass of rock,
120 feet high, has been penetrated by the sea to form a magnificent natural arch.

Steep-sided Ronas Voe cuts deeply into Northmavine Parish and its west coast. The district of North Roe lies north of Ronas Voe and is characterised by upland moorland, innumerable lochs and a string of scattered settlements along the eastern coastline.

159. "HEYLOR, RONAS VOE"
Heylor township is strung out along the southern shore of Ronas Voe, a fjord-like arm of the sea extending for about seven miles. Two Norwegian-owned whaling stations opened in Ronas Voe in 1903 but closed at the time of the First World War.

160. " 'SIXERNS', FEIDALAND, NORTH ROE"
Fethaland lies at the northernmost point of Mainland. Its location, although remote, was convenient for the haaf (deep sea) fishing grounds far out to sea, and the ruins of the lodges used by the fishermen are still to be seen. "Sixerns", boats with six oars, were once the most common fishing vessel and were specially developed for the haaf fishing.

BURRA ISLE
HAMNAVOE

Hamnavoe is an attractive fishing village on the island of West Burra. The islands of West and East Burra have been linked together by bridge since about 1791 but it was not until 1969 that work began on the project to link West Burra to Mainland via the intervening island of Trondra. The bridge scheme, estimated to cost £500,000, was completed in October 1971.

161. "HAMNAVOE"

Situated on one of Shetland's finest natural harbours, Hamnavoe grew, after about 1890, to become one of only two true villages in Shetland (the second was Scalloway but, of course, Sandwick and Brae have also developed into villages in more recent years). The fishing and boat-building industries have long been important in Hamnavoe.

FOR POSTAGE STAMP

Printed in Saxony

162. "HAMNAVOE"

Most of Hamnavoe's cottages date from the first quarter of the twentieth century. The rows of two-roomed cottages, many with ornate, often crenellated porches, were built largely for the local fishermen and their families.

BRESSAY

The island of Bressay, seven miles long by three miles wide, provides a picturesque back-drop to Lerwick, three-quarters of a mile to the west across Bressay Sound. Ward Hill (743 feet) dominates the island and the views are well worth the climb. Today, most of the island's 350 inhabitants live on the west side but, until the land was cleared for sheep in the 1870s, the population of over 900 (in 1841) lived mainly in crofting townships on the east.

163. "BRESSAY LIGHTHOUSE"
Bressay Lighthouse is always a welcome sight on approaching Lerwick and a sad one when departing. Built at Kirkabister Ness in 1858, the lighthouse, now automated, is adjacent to an impressive natural arch. The eroded cliffs at this south end of Bressay are impressive.

164. "CAVE OF THE BARD, BRESSAY"
An official guide book to Shetland in the 1920s states that "No visitor should miss seeing the Cave of the Bard, a trip, however, to be undertaken only in fine weather. A boat must be engaged, and excursionists should provide themselves with torches".

N O S S

The island of Noss lies due east of Bressay and is separated from its larger neighbour
by the narrow stretch of water called Noss Sound. Noss itself was home to about 20 people
in 1851 but lost its last inhabitants in 1939. The island was declared a National Nature Reserve
in 1955 and today is occupied in the summer months by the reserve's warden.

165. "BELOW THE NOUP, NOSS"
Noss rises steeply from west to east, reaching
592 feet at Noss Head. Pictured here, below the
sheer cliffs of the Noup which drop dramatically
to the sea, a spectacle best appreciated from
sea-level, is the Lerwick yacht, *Soldian*.

166. "A CORNER OF NOSS"
The red sandstone cliffs of Noss have been weathered
into a series of horizontal ledges. These are ideal
breeding grounds for countless Razorbills, Guillemots,
Kittiwakes and Gannets whilst many Puffins nest in
burrows near the top of the cliffs.

FAIR ISLE

Fair Isle is Shetland's southernmost island and, geographically, Britain's remotest inhabited island. It lies about 24 miles south-west of Sumburgh Head, roughly half way between Shetland and Orkney. The island is about three miles long by about one and a half wide and has a world-wide reputation as being the home of the famous "Fair Isle" knitwear.

SOUTH HARBOUR, FAIR ISLE

167. "SOUTH HARBOUR, FAIR ISLE"
Fair Isle's South Lighthouse (pictured) was built in 1891 (in the same year as the island's North Lighthouse) and is an imposing 85 feet high. The large white house to the right is Melville House (now called "Utra"), Fair Isle's post office when this photograph was taken.

NORTH HAVEN, FAIR ISLE   PHOTO J. D. RATTAR

168. "NORTH HAVEN, FAIR ISLE"
North Haven is the landing place and base for the island's mailboat, currently *Good Shepherd IV*. Fair Isle has been served by successive mailboats called *Good Shepherd* since 1921, the first being wrecked in North Haven itself in 1948. The first Fair Isle Bird Observatory opened at North Haven in 1948. The Observatory has justly become world famous in ornithological circles. The present Observatory building dates from 1969.

FAIR ISLE

Fair Isle's population reached a peak of 380 in 1861 but declined rapidly thereafter. When remote St Kilda was evacuated in 1930 Fair Isle's population was down to 108 and there were fears that Fair Isle, too, might cease to be a viable community. The island was acquired by the National Trust for Scotland in 1954 and many improvements took place. Since then the population has stabilised at about 70.

169. "POST OFFICE, FAIR ISLE"
A post office first opened on Fair Isle in February 1877. It was upgraded to a telegraph office eleven years later. The post office was located at Melville House (now known as "Utra") when this photograph was taken. It moved to its present location, at "Shirva", in 1948.

170. "FAIR ISLE"
Fair Isle's population live on the crofting lands occupying the southern half of the island. Sheep Craig (433 feet) is a well-known landmark and towers over the landscape. The larger of the two buildings to the upper left is the Methodist Chapel (built in 1886) and the smaller is now the George Waterston Memorial Centre, containing a wealth of material relating to Fair Isle's history.

F O U L A

Foula is the most westerly of the islands, situated about 14 miles from the nearest point on Mainland Shetland. Its five great hills also make Foula the most rugged of the islands, rising to 1373 feet at The Sneug, and give the island its distinctive shape when viewed from many parts of the Mainland. The Kame, a sheer drop of 1220 feet, is the second highest sea cliff in Britain.

FOULA "THE EDGE OF THE WORLD"

PHOTO WILLIAMSON, SCALLOWAY

171. "FOULA 'THE EDGE OF THE WORLD"
The title of C. J. Williamson's postcard refers to Michael Powell's film "The Edge of the World", shot on location on Foula in 1936. The film itself gave considerable national publicity to Foula when the film's director and his crew became stranded on the island for several weeks. "Film Party Marooned on Storm-Swept Island", said the *Daily Mail* headline, Michael Powell and his crew being victims of the unpredictable weather which has often made Foula Britain's most isolated inhabited island.

172. "EGG HUNTING, SHETLAND"
Seabirds' eggs, collected from the cliffs in early summer, were a source of food in several parts of Shetland. They were particularly important to the islanders of Foula, where seabirds still nest in their countless thousands. Despite the extreme danger involved, Foula's own resident author, Sheila Gear, states that "Contrary to the romantic thinking of some of our more dramatic writers of island tales, not many islanders lost their lives like this".

FOULA

Foula's isolation has had a dramatic effect on the island's population. The island was
home to 267 people in 1881 but this declined rapidly to the point where today the number
is below 50. Officialdom took the attitude that Foula would soon be left solely to the seabirds
and treatment of the island was characterised by neglect. It was only in the late 1980s that
the determination of the islanders was at last rewarded with a new electricity scheme,
a new school, harbour improvements and the promise of a new mailboat.

173. "HAM, FOULA"
Foula has long suffered from the lack of a safe, protected harbour. Ham Voe, on the
island's east side, is still the island's landing place. The pier in J. D. Rattar's photograph
was built by the island's owner in about 1910. Recent improvements to the harbour and
pier have been welcomed but it is still necessary for boats to be hauled on to
dry land to prevent their destruction at the hands of the sea.

174. "THE MAIL BOAT, FOULA"
A number of the islanders wait at Foula pier for the mailboat's departure. The boat's
mast, too, rests on the pier awaiting departure. The boat's oars testify to the likely arduous
nature of the long round trip to the village of Walls on the West Mainland. The mailboat in
the photograph is still performing a service today — as the roof for a garage in Lerwick!

Separated from Mainland Shetland by the mile-wide Sound of Papa, the island of
Papa Stour is noted for its deeply indented coastline. It boasts magnificent cliffs with
natural arches, rock stacks and some of Shetland's finest caves. The island's population
now stands at only 35, a huge decrease since the population peaked at over 380 in 1841.

175. "THE HORN OF PAPA"

"The Horn" was a well-known Shetland landmark. It was a large, prominent rock
formation on the headland between Hund Geo and Akers Geo on Papa Stour's
west side. The Horn itself crashed into the sea during a great storm in 1953.

176. "FUGLE AND LIRI SKERRY"

Shown on modern Ordnance Survey maps as "Fogla" and "Lyra" Skerries, these
small islands, off Papa Stour's west coast, are typical of the island's rugged coastline.
The isolated rock stack to the right is "The Snolda", pictured on the next page.

PAPA STOUR
PAPA STOUR AND THE VE SKERRIES

Shetland's enormously long coastline can be beautiful and awe-inspiring. It can be dramatic and, at times, it can be dangerous. Perhaps no stretch of the coastline illustrates these characteristics better than Papa Stour and its out-lying skerries.

177. "THE SNOLDIE"

The Snolda is a dramatic sea stack off Papa Stour's west coast. Its considerable height is shown to effect by the photographer's technique in adding the boat to the scene.

178. "BREAKER ON VEE SKERRIES"

The Ve Skerries is a dangerous reef consisting of several small rocky islands about three miles to the north-west of Papa Stour. Amongst other recorded incidents, it was the scene, in March 1930, of the tragic loss of the Aberdeen trawler "Ben Doran", which ran aground in fog. All attempts to rescue the crew were defeated by the mountainous seas breaking over the rocks and, tragically, all the crew perished. A lighthouse was built on the Ve Skerries in 1979.

WHALSAY

The island of Whalsay, about three miles east of Mainland, is something of a success
story as far as Shetland's outlying islands are concerned. Most rural parts of Shetland
have witnessed a marked population decline since the peak was recorded in the middle
years of the nineteenth century but Whalsay's population has increased by about a
third over the same period. Today, the island is home to about 1000 people.

Symbister, Whalsay, Shetland Isles   PN5520

179. "SYMBISTER, WHALSAY"
Symbister is Whalsay's main settlement. The island is dependent on fishing
and Symbister is now the base for some of Britain's most up-to-date fishing vessels.
Symbister House (centre) stands loftily on the hill overlooking the township. It was
built at considerable cost in the 1820s by the local landowner, Robert Bruce and,
having been converted in the 1940s, is now the island's junior high school.

180. "M.V. EARL OF ZETLAND PASSING SYMBISTER NESS LIGHT"
The second *Earl of Zetland* took over the Lerwick-North Isles service from the first
ship of the same name in 1939. She was requisitioned for war service but returned to the
North Isles run in 1946. The *Earl* was retired and the service withdrawn in February 1975
following the introduction of car ferries on the shorter inter-island routes. Today,
Symbister is linked by car ferry to Laxo in the Mainland Parish of Nesting.

YELL

Yell is the second largest of the Shetland group (after Mainland) and is about 17 miles north to south by about six miles west to east. Today's main road strikes across Yell's peat-covered moorland interior. This scenery might at first impression make the island seem rather bleak but Yell's coastal scenery is much more prepossessing and is deserving of the visitor's attention.

181. "LINKSHOUSE, MID YELL"
Situated on the sheltered south side of Mid Yell Voe on Yell's east coast, the township is now simply known as Mid Yell and is the natural centre of the island. Linkshouse is the name of the substantial merchant's house (dating from 1770) at the pierhead and the local post office's name was Linkshouse until this was changed to Mid Yell in the early 1880s. The small kirk of St John's (right) dates from 1832 and replaced an earlier church on the site of the burial ground (left) on the shoreline.

182. "SCATLANDS, WESTSANDWICK"
The modern road runs to the east of the crofting township of Westsandwick. The settlement's burial ground (centre) is on the west bank of the Loch of Scatlands. The land on the horizon is the North Roe district of the Mainland's northernmost parish, Northmavine.

YELL

Yell's population today stands at about 1100, rather less than half the numbers recorded when the island reached its population peak in 1871. In common with much of Shetland, its settlements are confined to the narrow, more fertile coastal areas.

183. "BURRAVOE, YELL"
Burravoe is the main settlement of the southern part of Yell and for many years was a port of call for the "Earl of Zetland" on the North Isles' passenger and freight service. Its oldest surviving house, built by local merchants, dates from 1672 and was restored in the late 1980s as a visitor centre.

184. "EPISCOPAL CHURCH AND POST OFFICE, BURRAVOE"
St Columba's Episcopal Church was built in 1900 and has been described as "A little rural gem . . . in Arts & Crafts gothic". Burravoe's first official post office was opened as long ago as 1839. The sender of this postcard was Dora Murly, a teacher at Mid Yell school.

98

YELL

The inter-island ferry from Yell to Unst departs from Gutcher on Yell's
north-east coast. Most visitors head straight for the ferry terminal and seem
to forget that much of interest in North Yell lies beyond.

185. "CULLIEVOE, YELL"

The crofting township of Cullivoe lies at the head of an arm of the sea also known as
Culli Voe. A few miles away is a memorial to the 58 men, largely from this district, who were
drowned in July 1881 when the fishing fleet was overtaken by a violent storm. It also serves
to remind us of the precarious footholds such remote rural communities often had.

186. "BLUE MULL FROM YELL"

Blue Mull is a rocky headland (centre) on the island of Unst. It lies due east from
this stretch of Yell's coastline, itself just north of Cullivoe. The headland, rising to 223
feet, gives its name to Bluemull Sound, the stretch of water separating Yell from Unst.

Unst, the northernmost island in the British Isles, has inspired postcard-producers
to use the ''Britain's most northerly . . .'' description since the earliest days of
postcard production. Lighthouse, village, hotel, house, post office and even
post-box, amongst others, have all received this distinction.

187. ''QUEEN'S HOTEL, BALTASOUND.
THE MOST NORTHERLY HOTEL IN THE UNITED KINGDOM''
The Queen's Hotel subsequently became the Hotel Nord but was still advertised as
''Britain's most Northerly Hotel''. Its facilities included ''Golf, Tennis, Picnics, Bathing, Boating
& Sea Fishing, Pictish & Norse Relics, Wonderful Cliff Scenery & Bird Life'' and a ''10,000
Acres Moor and Snipe Marshes''. The building still stands but is no longer a hotel.

188. ''BRITAIN'S MOST NORTHERLY POST OFFICE''
In 1960 Her Majesty The Queen visited Haroldswick post office (''Britain's most northerly'')
and sent a telegram to the Governor of Jersey at Samares post office (the most southerly).
Later, in July 1972, the Post Office gave recognition to Haroldswick's claim to fame and issued
· the local post office with a special ''Britain's Northernmost Post Office'' datestamp. At
least four later but similarly worded datestamps have been used at Haroldswick
and, happily, visitors' postcards still receive the special postmark.

UNST

BALTASOUND

The village of Baltasound is Unst's main settlement and lies halfway along the island's east coast. It is situated at the head of an arm of the sea (Balta Sound) sheltered by the uninhabited island of Balta. It was this sheltered position on Britain's northernmost island which led Baltasound to play such an important role in the herring fishery at the end of the nineteenth century.

189. "BALTASOUND HARBOUR"

Baltasound witnessed an astounding growth in the final few years of the nineteenth century when it became one of Britain's major herring ports. In 1902 it was even to beat Lerwick in terms of herring prodution. In this remarkable year there were over 650 boats based at Baltasound. The season itself was short (only about seven weeks) but during that time both sides of the voe were crowded with jetties and over 2000 gutters were temporarily accommodated in huts lining the waterfront.

Baltasound looking West   Photo J.D. Rattar

190. "BALTASOUND LOOKING WEST"

Although the herring industry declined rapidly after about 1905, the physical remains of the herring boom lingered in Baltasound for many years. Many of the temporary buildings and the wooden jetties still survived when J. D. Rattar visited in the 1920s.

U N S T

Unst is approximately 12 miles long by five miles wide. Its population of about 1000
is largely to be found in the four scattered crofting communities of Baltasound, Haroldswick,
Norwick and Uyeasound. The RAF base at Saxa Vord is today the island's main employer.
The base's modern structures lie adjacent to the wild and untamed scenery of the
Hermaness National Nature Reserve, a site of international importance and,
during the summer months, a home to countless thousands of seabirds.

BRITAIN'S MOST NORTHERLY DWELLING HOUSE, SKOW, SHETLAND

191. "BRITAIN'S MOST NORTHERLY DWELLING HOUSE, SKAW"
The house at Skaw, facing the lonely bay known as the Wick of Skaw, is Britain's most
northerly. In recent years it has been available for rent as self-catering accommodation but was
obviously a functioning croft when this photograph was taken in the 1950s. The last man to
speak the old Norn language of Shetland (derived from Old Norse) reputedly lived at Skaw.

Muness Castle, Unst, Shetland.

192. "MUNESS CASTLE, UNST"
Muness Castle is a magnificent ruin in an isolated area of south-east Unst,
not far from Uyeasound. It was built in 1598 for Laurence Bruce and was probably
designed by the same architect responsible for Scalloway Castle (built
two years later). The two castles have many features in common.

MUCKLE FLUGGA

About a mile north of the great headland of Herma Ness (where Hermaness Hill, the heart of the National Nature Reserve, rises to 657 feet) lie Muckle Flugga and Out Stack, the most northerly landfalls in the British Isles.

193. "MUCKLE FLUGGA LIGHTHOUSE AND OUTSTACK. MOST NORTHERLY POINT IN GREAT BRITAIN"

Muckle Flugga Lighthouse was completed in 1858 at a cost of £32,000. It was designed by David Stevenson, uncle of the writer Robert Louis Stevenson (whose signature is to be found in an old visitors' book). Today, we can only marvel at the feat of engineering required to build on top of a 200 foot rock pinnacle surrounded by dangerous seas. The Out Stack is called "Ootsta" locally.

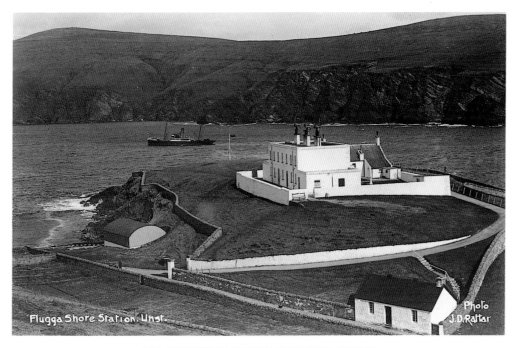

194. "FLUGGA SHORE STATION, UNST"

Muckle Flugga's shore station was built on The Ness at Burrafirth, on the north coast of Unst. The station's neat, white-washed, flat-topped keepers' accommodation is typical of the architecture of the Commissioners of Northern Lighthouses.

SHETLAND BIRDS

Shetland is a perfect place both for birds and for birdwatching. Of the 24 seabird species which breed in the British Isles, 21 breed in Shetland, many in large numbers. Over 40 other bird species also breed in the islands. No-one could fail to be awe-struck by the sight of the great cliffs of Hermaness, Noss, Foula or Fair Isle during the seabirds' breeding season.

195. "BIRDS OF SHETLAND"
Five different bird species, representative of the many species to be found in Shetland, are shown on this multi-view postcard. Although published by C. J. Williamson, the postcard's individual photographs were taken by W. Kay.

196. "PUFFINS"
Most people's favourite seabird is the Puffin, an attractive and colourful visitor to Shetland's cliffs during the summer months. In Shetland's local dialect the Puffin is known as the "Tammie Norie".

J. D. Rattar produced many different postcards from his superb bird photographs. Anyone interested both in Rattar's photographic work and in Shetland's birdlife could put together quite an extensive and attractive collection of his postcards.

197. "EIDER DUCK"

The Eider Duck — or "Dunter", to give it its local name — is fairly common throughout Shetland's coastal waters. Once her ducklings have hatched, the female Eider (pictured) can often be seen in small groups protecting the young of several females.

198. "RED-THROATED DIVER"

Known as the "Raingoose" in Shetland, the Red-Throated Diver breeds on isolated lochs throughout Shetland. Approximately 60% of the British population of these beautiful birds breed in Shetland.

Countless thousands have sailed away from Lerwick over many decades. Some left as emigrants to find a new life for their families in Britain's overseas Dominions. Some left to join the Royal Navy, the Merchant Navy or the Army. Some left on vessels to hunt the whale or seek out the herring shoals. Some, for various reasons, never managed to return. But for those fortunate enough to return, they were only too glad to see the old familiar landmarks of Shetland.

199. "BOATS LEAVING, LERWICK"
It was common enough for Shetland's womenfolk to watch their loved ones sail away, not knowing when they would return or if they would return at all.

200. "VISITORS LEAVING LERWICK"
Visitors, too, know the sadness of departure. Sailing southwards from Lerwick, most visitors, captured by the magic that is uniquely Shetland, vow that one day they will return!

ACKNOWLEDGEMENTS

The following is a list of the photographers or publishers whose postcards
are featured in this book. The numbers are those identifying each of the 200
postcards reproduced in the volume. Where no reference number is given,
the photographer or publisher of a particular postcard is not known.

CONOCHIE, W. K., Stationer, Lerwick — 4
DUNCAN, C. J., Lerwick — 64
GRAY, W. — 118
HARTMANN, F., Scotland — 41, 48, 105
INKSTER, A. F., Scalloway — 115
KENT, Tom, Kirkwall, Orkney — 67, 99
LESLIE, W., Dunrossness — 122
MANSON & Co., Hillswick — 152, 156
MANSON, T. & J., Lerwick — 184
MATHEWSON, T., Bookseller, Lerwick — 50, 111
MORRISON, H. & SON, Booksellers, Lerwick — 35, 104
NEWMAN — J., Glasgow — 21, 42, 134
RAMSAY, R. H., Lerwick — 9, 11, 24, 29, 36, 46, 47, 65, 66, 76, 84, 86, 89, 95, 103, 128, 154, 172
RATTAR, J. D., Lerwick — 7, 8, 10, 12, 17, 19, 34, 37, 44, 45, 49, 51-55, 57, 58, 61, 69, 70, 73-75, 79-81, 83, 88, 91, 96, 102, 106, 108, 112, 119-121, 123, 125-127, 129-131, 133, 135, 138-143, 145, 149, 150, 157-159, 163-168, 170, 173, 174, 176-178, 180-183, 185, 186, 190, 193, 194, 196-198, 200
SANDISON & Sons, Baltasound — 189
SHETLAND TIMES LIMITED, The — 32, 38, 60, 100, 124, 137
SINCLAIR, E., Shetland — 93
SMITH, R., Shetland — 117
TUCK, Raphael & Sons, England — 31, 77
VALENTINE & Sons Limited, Dundee — 5, 6, 13, 15, 18, 25, 27, 30, 59, 68, 71, 98, 161, 169, 192
WILLIAMSON, C. J., Scalloway — 2, 3, 16, 20, 26, 28, 43, 63, 72, 82, 97, 101, 109, 113, 114, 116, 146, 151, 162, 171, 195
WILLIAMSON, R., Lerwick — 14, 23, 39, 62
WILSON, George Washington, Aberdeen — 56, 85, 87

BIBLIOGRAPHY

DONALDSON, Gordon — *Northwards by Sea* (1978)
FINNIE, Mike — *Shetland: An Illustrated Architectural Guide* (1990)
GEAR, Sheila — *Foula, Island West of the Sun* (1983)
MacKAY, James A. — *Islands Postal History Series No.8: Shetland* (1979)
NICOLSON, James R. — *Shetland* (1979)
NICOLSON, James R. — *Traditional Life in Shetland* (1983)
ROYAL COMMISSION ON THE ANCIENT AND HISTORICAL MONUMENTS OF SCOTLAND — *Exploring Scotland's Heritage, Orkney & Shetland* (1985)
SIMMATH PRESS LIMITED, The — *Shetland Islands: Official Guide Book* (1920s)
SMITH, John S. — *George Washington Wilson in Orkney & Shetland* (1986)
ZETLAND EDUCATION COMMITTEE — *The Shetland Book* (Edited by A. T. Cluness) (1967)

C. J. WILLIAMSON
THE STUDIO - SCALLOWAY
SHETLAND

SOUVENIR POST CARD

POST ◇ CARD.